# THE BEAUTIFULLY ORGANIZED HOME PLANNER

Copyright ©2020 Nikki Boyd

Published by Paige Tate & Co.
Paige Tate & Co. is an imprint of Blue Star Press
PO Box 8835, Bend, OR 97708
contact@paigetate.com
www.paigetate.com

Writing by Nikki Boyd

Design by Chris Ramirez

ISBN 9781944515980

Printed in Colombia

11  10  9  8  7  6  5  4  3  2

# THE BEAUTIFULLY ORGANIZED HOME PLANNER

SIMPLE SYSTEMS AND WORKSHEETS
FOR MANAGING YOUR HOUSEHOLD

## NIKKI BOYD

CREATOR OF "AT HOME WITH NIKKI"

# TABLE OF CONTENTS

# FOREWORD

I spent *many* years of my life feeling like a complete failure. Everyday life skills just didn't come easily for me, and I felt as though I had somehow misplaced my "how to be an adult" instruction manual. I struggled to manage my finances, keep my home clean, arrive places on time, and remember all the little things required of a grown-up (like dentist appointments, my mom's birthday, and where the heck I put my car keys).

While other people in my life effortlessly juggled children, careers, and their tidy homes, I celebrated the rare occasions when I found a pair of matching socks in the morning. I was drowning in clutter, to-dos, and self-pity, and I was desperate for a way out. While others seemed to casually stroll down the path of life, I was hacking my way through it with a dull machete.

I read endless self-help books and watched countless videos from every lifestyle guru I could find. I was shocked to discover that the underlying message was *always* the same. While there wasn't a "quick fix" to all my life's problems, there was one simple solution that would make every aspect better. *Are you ready for it?* Disclaimer: The secret to success isn't nearly as cool or elusive as you may think, and you are probably already doing it to some degree. It's having a plan and writing down the steps to achieve it.

Before you roll your eyes, hear me out. Planning will have more impact on your success than any other action you can take in your life. I am *not* just talking about having a basic plan like, *"I'm going to organize my home!"* (though that is a great goal). A true plan is so much more than that. President Dwight D. Eisenhower said it best when he said, "Plans are useless, but planning is indispensable." The *real* secret is understanding how to break down your goals into easy and actionable steps that you can achieve with minimal effort. Planning your life is like paving the path to your end goal (no dull machete required).

Real planning skills take time and experience to master. On my journey down the path towards a happier and more successful life, I've discovered many incredible people who have been my guide and inspiration, but none more than Nikki Boyd. Nikki embodies everything that I want to be: kind, loving, organized, successful, and effortlessly polished. She truly lives an inspiring life, while offering support and wisdom to her many followers like me.

Nikki's first book, *Beautifully Organized*, was a masterpiece with its perfect combination of educational advice and stunning beauty. Now, Nikki is offering us a glimpse into how she achieved such a beautifully organized home by sharing her incredible organizational planning tools with us. This book is the roadmap to success, already designed and created, with her proven methods and planning pages. By taking the hard work out of creating the plan, Nikki is giving us a jump start to the beautifully organized home we all deserve.

I'm truly honored to be writing the foreword for one of my greatest mentors. I'm also so grateful to be a small part of *your* journey towards success as well. Nikki's wisdom, motivation, and planning will help us all achieve the home and the life of our dreams.

CAS AARSSEN

Bestselling Author of *Real Life Organizing* and *Cluttered Mess to Organized Success*

# INTRODUCTION

One of my favorite movies is Mary Poppins because the magical nanny, one woman, is able to walk into a home and immediately create a fun and adventurous atmosphere that births happiness into struggling households.

I like to think of myself as the Mary Poppins of home organization. It is my life's mission to help families live beautifully in their homes, and just like Mary Poppins, I have my big bag of tricks to accomplish my mission. And now I'm sharing them with you together in one place with this planner!

In my first book, *Beautifully Organized: A Guide to Function and Style in Your Home,* I mapped out five essential steps to an organized home. The reader response was incredible. It was an honor to see how many families I could help by sharing the knowledge I've gained as a professional organizer. I immediately wanted to do more!

My goal with this planner is to provide you with the tactical tools you need to create systems that work and bring order, calm, and strong communication to your household. You'll find tips and simple worksheets for everything from having productive family meetings, planning for emergencies, keeping your home clean and well-maintained, staying on top of school schedules and responsibilities, implementing a fool-proof paper filing system, and creating a household budget that helps you maximize your savings. These are the lifelong systems that every home needs to run efficiently.

This home-life planner is your life-changing tool for getting your home essentials in place. Your beautiful, happy, and well-organized home is right around the corner. So grab a cup of coffee, and let's get started!

# AFFIRM MY HOME

My home is free from clutter.
It is essential for me to keep my home clutter-free
in order to create a peaceful environment where I can live, work, and rest.

Living in a disorganized space leads to more chaos, which can turn
into an emotional burden. I free myself from the bonds of disarray by
establishing order in my life.

Each day, I set aside 15 minutes to sort
through areas prone to clutter, such as a mail basket or a closet.
It feels good to keep things tidy.

I keep my home organized because
I enjoy finding things quickly when I need them. Removing clutter
from my home allows me to find items with ease. The reward
of living in a clean environment far outweighs the cost of cleaning up.

Creating a clean space demands that I rid myself of unnecessary items.
The strength required to throw away items that are of no real
value is found within me. I am merciless when it comes to tossing
the clutter. When I have a hard time parting with an item,
I remind myself that memories, not possessions, have value.

Keeping my home tidy entails a time investment. I am willing to
devote time each day to organizing. I fight against discouragement
and setbacks by celebrating my progress.

Today, I choose to create
a plan for change. I sort through my clutter and throw away any items
that are simply taking up space. With determination,
I develop a system to maintain a clean living area.

# ESSENTIAL №1

## FAMILY MEETINGS

In my first book, *Beautifully Organized*, I discussed the importance of incorporating a tool for increasing good communication with your family. It is so important for the entire family to be on the same page to ensure that you have a well-run home. Holding regular family meetings is the perfect way to come together and get everyone in sync. If systems and expectations are not clearly and regularly communicated, then it's all too easy for your family to get off track.

I also believe in what I call a "family mission statement." This is a way for your whole family to agree on shared values, and is a great foundation for your family meetings. I've included tips and worksheets for creating a mission statement in this chapter. You may decide if this exercise is useful to you. It's totally optional—and likely depends on the stage and size of your family!

TIP

*Bring your family mission statement to every meeting to remind your family members of their purpose before you discuss other matters.*

## FAMILY MISSION STATEMENT

Having a shared vision of your family's values is essential to strengthening the bond between all family members and to ensuring a well-established home environment. A family mission statement is a collaborative understanding between your family members of how your family wants to be identified, and the principles you live by. It keeps the entire family focused on your principles and bonds you as a unit. Use the Values & Purpose List (pages 13-14) to agree on family values, then use the Mission Statement Worksheet (pages 16-17) to draft your statement.

## THE AGENDA

The key to success for any meeting is an agenda. The great thing about an agenda is that it doesn't have to change from week to week. You can follow the same agenda each week, which provides consistency for the family. Use the Family Home Meeting Agenda (page 19) to plan your family's meetings.

## FAMILY CALENDAR AND MEAL PLANNER

A family calendar is a wonderful tool to keep track of everyone's schedule in one consolidated location. It enables you to see any schedule conflicts, and provides everyone with an understanding (and potentially compassion) for all family members' schedules. Make copies of the Family Home Calendar worksheet (page 20) to organize your family's weekly schedule. I have also provided a Meal Planner worksheet (page 21) to help you plan your family's weekly meals ahead of time. Use your Family Calendar to assess how busy your upcoming week might be and then plan meals that fit into your family's schedule and lifestyle.

## FAMILY NEEDS

As a family unit there are always needs: home items that need to be stocked, supplies for a special school project, etc. Week after week we scramble to stay on top of things. After a long day of work, no one wants to hear those words, "I need..." You can resolve this by discussing all needs for the family at one time in your weekly family meetings. Then you can go into your week prepared. Make copies of the Family Home Needs worksheet (page 22) to track your family's needs each week.

## HOME ISSUES

Your family meeting is also a time to address any problems in the home, such as maintenance concerns and the distribution of housekeeping responsibilities. Pinpointing issues together as a family allows you to keep your home running well and the people who live there happy. Make copies of the Family Home Issues worksheet (page 23) to keep track of issues in your home that require attention. Use this page to identify any issues, and the family members responsible for resolving them. During the following home meetings, check in with your family members about their progress.

# VALUE & PURPOSE

## LIST

### SELECT AND VOTE ON YOUR FAMILY'S VALUES AND PURPOSE

| | | | |
|---|---|---|---|
| Dependability | Motivation | Harmony | Helpfulness |
| Reliability | Positivity | Growth | Accessibility |
| Acceptance | Adaptability | Happiness | Community |
| Correctness | Achievement | Will | Intelligence |
| Commitment | Fitness | Power | Meditation |
| Open-mindedness | Courage | Leadership | Understanding |
| Consistency | Ambition | Contribution | Affluence |
| Honesty | Perseverance | Liberation | Truth |
| Efficiency | Control | Flexibility | Idealism |
| Assertiveness | Influence | Connection | Devotion |
| Accuracy | Patriotism | Integrity | Loyalty |
| Good humor | Service to others | Love | Appreciation |
| Compassion | Environmentalism | Awareness | Caring |
| Spirit of adventure | Camaraderie | Healing | Artistry |

| | | | |
|---|---|---|---|
| Approachability | Optimism | Cleanliness | Hygiene |
| Playfulness | Respect | Grace | Fun |
| Carefulness | Knowledge | Closeness | Generosity |
| Prosperity | Affection | Joy | Individuality |
| Kindness | Alertness | Making a difference | Imagination |
| Abundance | Honor | Consciousness | Confidence |
| Focus | Brilliance | Conviction | Obedience |
| Doing | Innovation | Frugality | Patience |
| Professionalism | Wisdom | Hospitality | Peace |
| Conservation | Bravery | Amusement | Heart accomplishment |
| Creativity | Charm | Education | Financial independence |
| Passion | Boldness | Vision | |
| Acknowledgment | Change | Calmness | |
| Activeness | Friendship | Impartiality | |

| CHOSEN VALUES | STATEMENT |
| --- | --- |
| Dependability | Be dependable in everything we do |
| Honesty | Honesty is a must |
| Creativity | Nurture creativity |
| Happiness | Happiness is everything |
| Growth | Always find ways to grow |
| Respect | Respect others |
| Confidence | Walk in confidence at all times |
| Peace | Bring peace to all situations |
| Playfulness | Always find time for playfulness |
| Love | Love each other |

### SAMPLE STATEMENT

Our family's mission is to be dependable in everything we do, knowing that honesty is a must. We will nurture creativity and always find ways to grow. Respecting others and bringing peace to all situations is our top priority. We will love each other and know that happiness is everything.

# FAMILY MISSION STATEMENT

It is important to have a solid mission statement for your family—one that truly defines your mission and purpose as a family unit. Answer the following questions as a family to get started on creating yours.

**WHAT ARE EIGHT TO TEN WORDS THAT DESCRIBE OUR FAMILY?**

_____  _____  _____  _____  _____

_____  _____  _____  _____  _____

**WHAT KIND OF RELATIONSHIP DO WE WANT TO HAVE WITH EACH OTHER?**

**WHAT IS UNIQUE ABOUT OUR FAMILY?**

**WHAT DOES OUR FAMILY LOVE DOING TOGETHER?**

WHAT ARE THE PRINCIPLES ON WHICH WE WANT OUR FAMILY TO BE BASED?

_____

_____

_____

WHAT ARE THREE THINGS WE NEED TO CHANGE IN OUR FAMILY?

_____

_____

_____

HOW DO WE WANT TO TREAT EACH OTHER?

_____

_____

_____

WHAT DO WE WANT OTHER PEOPLE TO SAY ABOUT OUR FAMILY?

_____

_____

_____

WHAT WORLD ISSUES DO WE WANT OUR FAMILY TO HAVE THE MOST IMPACT ON?

_____

_____

_____

TIP

*Use family photos to spark conversations about your family's mission. You can gain a lot of information from a photograph, such as your family's favorite activities, or experiences that have made your family passionate about certain things.*

# OUR FAMILY

## MISSION STATEMENT

FAMILY MEMBER

FAMILY MEMBER

FAMILY MEMBER

FAMILY MEMBER

FAMILY MEMBER

FAMILY MEMBER

FAMILY MEMBER

FAMILY MEMBER

FAMILY MEMBER

FAMILY MEMBER

FAMILY MEMBER

FAMILY MEMBER

# FAMILY HOME MEETING

## AGENDA

### FAMILY SCHEDULE

Discuss family member schedules for the coming week (practices, appointments, lessons, etc.) A general family calendar helps keep everyone on the same page.

### MEAL PLANNING

Discuss meal plans for the coming week, taking family member preferences and individual schedules into account.

### HOME ISSUES

Discuss any issues related to the home, including maintenance concerns and distribution of house-keeping responsibilities.

### SUCCESSES & STRUGGLES

Keep communication flowing within the family. Have each family member discuss one success and one struggle from the previous week.

### HOME NEEDS

Create a list of needs for the week. This might include things like field trip money, home products, supplies for school projects, etc.

### TEACHING TIME

Discuss a topic that is important to your family, such as faith, current events, family traditions, or life skills.

# FAMILY

## CALENDAR

WEEK OF _____

| MONDAY | TUESDAY | WEDNESDAY | THURSDAY | FRIDAY |
|--------|---------|-----------|----------|--------|
|  |  |  |  |  |

20

**SATURDAY**

**SUNDAY**

# FAMILY

## MEAL PLANNING

WEEK OF _____

| MONDAY | TUESDAY | WEDNESDAY | THURSDAY | FRIDAY |
|--------|---------|-----------|----------|--------|
|        |         |           |          |        |

### SATURDAY

### SUNDAY

# FAMILY

## HOME NEEDS

### FAMILY MEMBER

- _____
- _____
- _____
- _____
- _____
- _____

### FAMILY MEMBER

- _____
- _____
- _____
- _____
- _____
- _____

### FAMILY MEMBER

- _____
- _____
- _____
- _____
- _____
- _____

### FAMILY MEMBER

- _____
- _____
- _____
- _____
- _____
- _____

### FAMILY MEMBER

- _____
- _____
- _____
- _____
- _____
- _____

### FAMILY MEMBER

- _____
- _____
- _____
- _____
- _____
- _____

# FAMILY

## HOME ISSUES

| ISSUE | FAMILY MEMBER | ACCOUNTABILITY |
|-------|---------------|----------------|
| _____ | | ○ ○ |
| _____ | | ○ ○ |
| _____ | | |
| _____ | | ○ ○ |
| _____ | | ○ ○ |
| _____ | | |
| _____ | | ○ ○ |
| _____ | | ○ ○ |
| _____ | | |
| _____ | | ○ ○ |
| _____ | | ○ ○ |
| _____ | | |
| _____ | | ○ ○ |
| _____ | | ○ ○ |

# ESSENTIAL №2

## FAMILY EMERGENCY PREPAREDNESS PLAN

It is very important to establish a family emergency plan for your household. Often, we don't realize this until a disaster happens—which is not good planning! That is why I always encourage families to put a plan in place before disaster strikes.

It doesn't take long to accomplish this task, which is one that can save your family future heartache and difficulty during an emergency. Simply complete the following pages and then store your emergency plan where it is easy to grab.

# CREATING AN EMERGENCY PLAN

## 1

**STEP ONE:** RECORD FAMILY MEMBER & EMERGENCY CONTACTS

In today's society, our mobile phones are everything. Everywhere we go, they go. The issue when it comes to an emergency is that a mobile phone can experience technical difficulties during an emergency situation. Your phone may lose charge or get lost, leaving you without vital information for telephone numbers. Writing down this information in your emergency plan ensures that you will be able to access your emergency contacts during a disaster.

Complete the Family Members Contact Information worksheet (page 29) and Emergency and Medical Contacts worksheet (pages 30-32) to capture this important information for the essential people you may need to reach in the event of an emergency. This may include doctors, schools, employers, and your close family friends.

## 2

**STEP TWO:** DETERMINE AN EMERGENCY ACTION PLAN

What happens in the event of an emergency? How will you find each other? Where will you meet? What actions will you take?

Complete the Emergency Action Plan worksheet (page 33) with your family and verbally discuss to ensure that everyone knows and understands the plan.

## 3

**STEP THREE:** CREATE AN EMERGENCY KIT

I encourage every family to set up an emergency kit. This is also a great task to implement in your family weekly meeting. Incorporating every family member in the process can help everyone understand what is available in the emergency kit, as well as provide another opportunity to ensure the family understands your household's emergency plan.

Use the Emergency Kit Checklist (pages 34-35) to ensure that your emergency kit is in place and provides all the necessities to assist your family in the event of a disaster situation.

**4** **STEP FOUR:** RECORD INSURANCE PROVIDERS CONTACT INFORMATION

The purpose of the emergency plan is to simplify the process of resolving issues during a disaster. Having your insurance company contact information easily available can reduce your stress during a difficult time. This information should also stay current in your emergency plan. Complete the Insurance Providers Contact Information worksheet (pages 36-37) to track all insurance providers for your life, home, property, and automobiles for all family members. (See Chapter 6 for how to safely file and store this form.)

**5** **STEP FIVE:** CREATE A HOME INVENTORY LIST

It is important to keep track of your home inventory in the event of an emergency. This will make dealing with insurance companies a less painful experience. Completing your home inventory as a family can make the job much easier! Assign each family member the responsibility for logging one space in the home. Keep this inventory list with all of your other emergency plan information. (See Chapter 6 for details.) Use the Home Inventory Log (pages 38-39) to track the items for each room of your home.

# 6 STEP SIX: CREATE FAMILY MEMBER PROFILES

It is heartbreaking to witness a family struggle to find their loved ones after a disaster. By completing a family profile on each family member, you have all of the necessary information needed to notify the public about your family member at a moment's notice. Complete an Adult Family Member Profile (pages 40-41) or Child Family Member Profile (pages 42-43) for each family member. Make additional copies as needed depending on the size of your family. When choosing or taking a photo, make sure it is a recent close-up photograph. (See chapter 6 for how to carefully file this information.)

---

**TIP**

*Remember, pets are important family members too. Be sure to complete a profile for them as well (pages 44-45).*

# FAMILY MEMBERS

## CONTACT INFORMATION

### FAMILY MEMBERS' NAMES AND CONTACT NUMBER

_____    \_\_\_\_\_ - \_\_\_\_\_ - \_\_\_\_\_

_____    \_\_\_\_\_ - \_\_\_\_\_ - \_\_\_\_\_

_____    \_\_\_\_\_ - \_\_\_\_\_ - \_\_\_\_\_

_____    \_\_\_\_\_ - \_\_\_\_\_ - \_\_\_\_\_

_____    \_\_\_\_\_ - \_\_\_\_\_ - \_\_\_\_\_

_____    \_\_\_\_\_ - \_\_\_\_\_ - \_\_\_\_\_

_____    \_\_\_\_\_ - \_\_\_\_\_ - \_\_\_\_\_

_____    \_\_\_\_\_ - \_\_\_\_\_ - \_\_\_\_\_

_____    \_\_\_\_\_ - \_\_\_\_\_ - \_\_\_\_\_

_____    \_\_\_\_\_ - \_\_\_\_\_ - \_\_\_\_\_

_____    \_\_\_\_\_ - \_\_\_\_\_ - \_\_\_\_\_

_____    \_\_\_\_\_ - \_\_\_\_\_ - \_\_\_\_\_

# EMERGENCY AND MEDICAL

## CONTACTS

NAME _____

HOME _____

ADDRESS _____

_____

_____

EMAIL _____

WORK # _____

MOBILE # _____

NOTES _____

_____


NAME _____

HOME _____

ADDRESS _____

_____

EMAIL _____

WORK # _____

MOBILE # _____

NOTES _____

_____

NAME _____

HOME _____

ADDRESS _____

_____

_____

EMAIL _____

WORK # _____

MOBILE # _____

NOTES _____

_____


NAME _____

HOME _____

ADDRESS _____

_____

EMAIL _____

WORK # _____

MOBILE # _____

NOTES _____

_____

# EMERGENCY AND MEDICAL

## CONTACTS

NAME ——————————————— EMAIL ———————————————

HOME ——————————————— WORK # ———————————————

ADDRESS ——————————————— MOBILE # ———————————————

——————————————— NOTES ———————————————

——————————————— ———————————————

NAME ——————————————— EMAIL ———————————————

HOME ——————————————— WORK # ———————————————

ADDRESS ——————————————— MOBILE # ———————————————

——————————————— NOTES ———————————————

——————————————— ———————————————

NAME ——————————————— EMAIL ———————————————

HOME ——————————————— WORK # ———————————————

ADDRESS ——————————————— MOBILE # ———————————————

——————————————— NOTES ———————————————

——————————————— ———————————————

NAME ——————————————— EMAIL ———————————————

HOME ——————————————— WORK # ———————————————

ADDRESS ——————————————— MOBILE # ———————————————

——————————————— NOTES ———————————————

——————————————— ———————————————

# EMERGENCY AND MEDICAL

## CONTACTS

NAME _____  EMAIL _____

HOME _____  WORK # _____

ADDRESS _____  MOBILE # _____

_____  NOTES _____

_____  _____


NAME _____  EMAIL _____

HOME _____  WORK # _____

ADDRESS _____  MOBILE # _____

_____  NOTES _____

_____  _____


NAME _____  EMAIL _____

HOME _____  WORK # _____

ADDRESS _____  MOBILE # _____

_____  NOTES _____

_____  _____


NAME _____  EMAIL _____

HOME _____  WORK # _____

ADDRESS _____  MOBILE # _____

_____  NOTES _____

_____  _____

# EMERGENCY

## ACTION PLAN

### FAMILY MEETING PLACE IN THE HOME
(SUDDEN EMERGENCY)

_____

_____

_____

### FAMILY MEETING PLACE
(IF WE CANNOT ACCESS HOME)

_____

_____

_____

### CHECKLIST

- TAKE PICTURES/VIDEO OF THINGS OF VALUE IN EACH ROOM
- SHUT OFF UTILITIES
- REACH OUT TO CONTACTS
- GET EMERGENCY KIT
- CHECK RADIO/TV FOR EVACUATION INSTRUCTIONS

### IMPORTANT NUMBERS

SHELTER INFORMATION _____

_____

_____

POISON CONTROL _____

_____

_____

EMERGENCY: DIAL 911

# EMERGENCY KIT

## CHECKLIST

### ESSENTIALS

- WATER (1 GALLON PER PERSON PER DAY)
- FIRST AID KIT, FRESHLY STOCKED
- CAN OPENER (NON-ELECTRIC)
- FLASHLIGHT
- ESSENTIAL MEDICATIONS
- BABY SUPPLIES (DIAPERS, WIPES, FORMULA, ETC.)
- DUFFLE BAG
- FUEL CONTAINER
- BUTANE LIGHTER
- EMERGENCY CONTACT SHEET
- WATER PURIFICATION KIT
- FIRST AID BOOK
- NONPERISHABLE FOODS
- BLANKETS/SLEEPING BAG
- PORTABLE RADIO
- BATTERIES
- PET SUPPLIES (INCLUDING WATER)
- WIPES
- CLEAN CLOTHES
- WHISTLE
- LOCAL MAP
- CASH / COINS
- MOBILE PHONE AND CHARGER
- EYEGLASSES

### SAFETY AND COMFORT

- STURDY SHOES
- HEAVY GLOVES FOR CLEARING DEBRIS
- CANDLES
- WATERPROOF MATCHES
- LIGHT STICKS
- MOIST TOWELETTES
- NONPRESCRIPTION MEDICATIONS (IBUPROFEN, ANTIDIARRHEAL, ETC.)
- KNIFE
- RAZOR BLADES
- TENT
- PONCHOS
- SEWING KIT
- TRASH BAGS
- BOOKS AND GAMES FOR CHILDREN

### COOKING

- PLASTIC KNIVES / SPOONS / FORKS
- PAPER PLATES / CUPS / TOWELS
- HEAVY-DUTY ALUMINUM FOIL
- CAMPING STOVE

# EMERGENCY KIT

## CHECKLIST

### SANITATION

- BAR SOAP
- ANTIBACTERIAL SOAP
- TOILET PAPER
- TOOTHBRUSHES
- TOOTHPASTE
- LIQUID DETERGENT
- COMB / BRUSH
- SHAMPOO
- FEMININE HYGIENE SUPPLIES

### IMPORTANT PAPERS

- BIRTH CERTIFICATES
- BANK INFORMATION
- CREDIT CARD
- PASSPORTS
- LAND TITLES
- MARRIAGE LICENSES
- INSURANCE FORMS
- SOCIAL SECURITY CARDS
- WILL(S)

### TOOLS AND SUPPLIES

- AX
- BROOM
- HAMMER
- PLASTIC TAPE
- DUCT TAPE
- STAPLE GUN
- SHOVEL
- PLIERS
- COIL OF HALF-INCH (0.5") ROPE

### OTHER

# INSURANCE PROVIDERS

## CONTACT INFORMATION

INSURANCE NAME _____

WEBSITE _____

ADDRESS _____

EMAIL _____

CONTACT NUMBER_____

POLICY NUMBER_____

NOTES

INSURANCE NAME _____

WEBSITE _____

ADDRESS _____

EMAIL _____

CONTACT NUMBER_____

POLICY NUMBER_____

NOTES

# INSURANCE PROVIDERS

INSURANCE NAME _____

WEBSITE _____

ADDRESS _____

EMAIL _____

CONTACT NUMBER _____

POLICY NUMBER _____

NOTES

INSURANCE NAME _____

WEBSITE _____

ADDRESS _____

EMAIL _____

CONTACT NUMBER _____

POLICY NUMBER _____

NOTES

# HOME

## INVENTORY LOG

ROOM _____    LAST UPDATED _____

| QTY | ITEM | DESCRIPTION | PURCHASE DATE |
|-----|------|-------------|---------------|
|     |      |             |               |
|     |      |             |               |
|     |      |             |               |
|     |      |             |               |
|     |      |             |               |
|     |      |             |               |
|     |      |             |               |
|     |      |             |               |
|     |      |             |               |
|     |      |             |               |
|     |      |             |               |
|     |      |             |               |

| MAKE / MODEL | SERIAL NUMBER | PRICE PAID |
|---|---|---|
| | | |
| | | |
| | | |
| | | |
| | | |
| | | |
| | | |
| | | |
| | | |
| | | |
| | | |
| | | |

# FAMILY MEMBER

## PROFILE

NAME _____

BIRTH DATE _____ GENDER _____

ADDRESS _____

CITY / STATE / ZIP _____

CELL PHONE _____

HOME NUMBER _____

ETHNICITY _____

HEIGHT _____ WEIGHT _____

EYE COLOR _____ HAIR COLOR _____

BIRTHMARKS / SCARS _____

BLOOD TYPE _____

ALLERGIES _____

MEDICATIONS _____

OTHER SPECIAL NEEDS _____

PLACE OF EMPLOYMENT _____

WORK ADDRESS _____

CITY / STATE / ZIP _____

SUPERVISOR NAME _____

NOTES _____

CLOSE-UP
IMAGE
OF
FAMILY
MEMBER
HERE

# FAMILY MEMBER

## PROFILE

NAME _____

BIRTH DATE _____ GENDER _____

ADDRESS _____

CITY / STATE / ZIP _____

CELL PHONE _____

HOME NUMBER _____

ETHNICITY _____

HEIGHT _____ WEIGHT _____

EYE COLOR _____ HAIR COLOR _____

BIRTHMARKS / SCARS _____

BLOOD TYPE _____

ALLERGIES _____

MEDICATIONS _____

OTHER SPECIAL NEEDS _____

PLACE OF EMPLOYMENT _____

WORK ADDRESS _____

CITY / STATE / ZIP _____

SUPERVISOR NAME _____

NOTES _____

CLOSE-UP
IMAGE
OF
FAMILY
MEMBER
HERE

# CHILD FAMILY MEMBER

## PROFILE

NAME _____

BIRTH DATE _____ GENDER _____

ADDRESS _____

CITY / STATE / ZIP _____

CELL PHONE _____

HOME NUMBER _____

ETHNICITY _____

HEIGHT _____ WEIGHT _____

EYE COLOR _____ HAIR COLOR _____

BIRTHMARKS / SCARS _____

BLOOD TYPE _____

ALLERGIES _____

MEDICATIONS _____

OTHER SPECIAL NEEDS _____

SCHOOL / DAYCARE _____

SCHOOL / DAYCARE ADDRESS _____

CITY / STATE / ZIP _____

PHONE NUMBER _____

TEACHER / CARETAKER'S NAME _____

NOTES _____

CLOSE-UP
IMAGE
OF
FAMILY
MEMBER
HERE

# CHILD FAMILY MEMBER

## PROFILE

NAME _____

BIRTH DATE _____ GENDER _____

ADDRESS _____

CITY / STATE / ZIP _____

CELL PHONE _____

HOME NUMBER _____

ETHNICITY _____

HEIGHT _____ WEIGHT _____

EYE COLOR _____ HAIR COLOR _____

BIRTHMARKS / SCARS _____

BLOOD TYPE _____

ALLERGIES _____

MEDICATIONS _____

OTHER SPECIAL NEEDS _____

SCHOOL / DAYCARE _____

SCHOOL / DAYCARE ADDRESS _____

CITY / STATE / ZIP _____

PHONE NUMBER _____

TEACHER / CARETAKER'S NAME _____

NOTES _____

CLOSE-UP
IMAGE
OF
FAMILY
MEMBER
HERE

# PET

## PROFILE

PET NAME _____

AGE _____

GENDER _____

BREED _____

EYE COLOR _____

FUR / FEATHER COLOR _____

DISTINCTIVE MARKINGS _____

MICROCHIP ID NUMBER _____

MICROCHIP REGISTERED WITH _____

ALLERGIES _____

SURGERIES _____

MEDICATIONS _____

OTHER SPECIAL NEEDS _____

BOARDER / PET SITTER _____

BOARDER'S ADDRESS _____

CITY / STATE / ZIP _____

PHONE NUMBER _____

VETERINARIAN _____

EMERGENCY VETERINARY CLINIC _____

NOTES _____

_____

CLOSE-UP
IMAGE
OF
PET
HERE

# PET

## PROFILE

PET NAME _____

AGE _____

GENDER _____

BREED _____

EYE COLOR _____

FUR / FEATHER COLOR _____

DISTINCTIVE MARKINGS _____

MICROCHIP ID NUMBER _____

MICROCHIP REGISTERED WITH _____

ALLERGIES _____

SURGERIES _____

MEDICATIONS _____

OTHER SPECIAL NEEDS _____

BOARDER / PET SITTER _____

BOARDER'S ADDRESS _____

CITY / STATE / ZIP _____

PHONE NUMBER _____

VETERINARIAN _____

EMERGENCY VETERINARY CLINIC _____

NOTES _____

_____

CLOSE-UP

IMAGE

OF

PET

HERE

# ESSENTIAL №3

# MAINTENANCE

Owning a home is a huge responsibility, and without a system in place to manage the mainte-nance of a home, the responsibility can become even greater and more costly.

A home maintenance schedule can save you a lot of money and stress when it comes to your home. Many families only address maintenance when a problem arises, which can often be in-convenient, stressful, and costly. Taking a more proactive approach to maintaining your home is important for several reasons, including:

- INCREASING AND MAINTAINING THE VALUE OF YOUR HOME
- AVOIDING THE COST OF UNEXPECTED MAINTENANCE REPAIRS
- REDUCING STRESS OF URGENT HOME REPAIRS
- AVOIDING WARRANTY ISSUES

# TRACKING YOUR HOME'S MAINTENANCE

### SEASONAL HOME MAINTENANCE CHECKLIST

These checklists (pages 50-53) keep all your maintenance needs categorized by season to help you easily keep your home maintained. It is important to review your maintenance checklist at the start of each season so that you can schedule any necessary appointments or tasks and plan any big expenses in advance. The items might not all apply to you depending on where you live and the design of your house. Feel free to add additional tasks unique to your home in the blank spaces provided.

### HOME MAINTENANCE CALENDAR

Make a copy each year of the Home Maintenance Calendar worksheet (pages 54-55) to list and track your home's maintenance requirements and share with your family.

### SERVICE PROVIDER CONTACT LOG

Service providers play a huge role in helping us maintain our homes. Although many home maintenance tasks are easy to do yourself, some tasks require professional assistance. Use the Service Provider Contact Log (pages 56-57) to keep track of all home service providers by category.

### HOME PROJECT SHEET

Do you ever feel like there is always something that needs to be fixed, decluttered, or rearranged in your home? Well, you are not alone. This is the reality in just about every home. The key to success in accomplishing your mission (as with most things) is to have a strategy.

Planning your projects can give you the motivation and drive to get started, as well as assist you in working out the particulars, such as budget, action items, and timelines. Make copies of the Home Project worksheet (pages 58-59) to organize and accomplish your home project goals.

## PAINT COLOR TRACKER

Painting your home is often the easiest and most budget-friendly way to enhance your home in little time. It is also very DIY-friendly.

It's important to keep track of the paint colors you use in your home. You may need to do touch-ups after a few years or reference a paint color for another space. Tracking how much paint is required to paint an area is also valuable information for future projects. Use the Paint Color Tracker worksheet (pages 60-64) to log your paint chips/cards and to document the brand, color, and quantity of paint needed for each room. Feel free to copy and fill in additional pages as needed!

## HOME HISTORY LOG

The items in our home play a huge role in the ease of our day-to-day lives.

A Home History Log (pages 65-70) tracks the life-span of the items in your home and can give you a heads-up on when you may need to replace them. It's very important to track this information so that you can be financially prepared and budget for these items.

## VEHICLE MAINTENANCE

We need our automobiles to come through for us every day, and keeping them in shape is how we make sure they do. While we have the convenience of receiving automatic notices from our automobile service center, it is still important to track for your own personal records, because a car is a tremendous investment. Use the Vehicle Maintenance Log (page 71) to easily track the health of your car and when it needs to be serviced.

---

TIP

*Another simple way to keep track of the paint color in a room is to write the brand and paint color on the back of the light switch plate in that specific room.*

# SEASONAL HOME MAINTENANCE

## CHECKLIST

### FALL

- VACUUM AND CLEAN VENTS
- CLEAN GARBAGE DISPOSAL
- CHECK CARBON MONOXIDE, SMOKE DETECTORS, AND FIRE EXTINGUISHERS
- CLEAN RANGE HOOD FILTERS
- INSPECT AND CHANGE HVAC FILTERS
- CHECK WATER SOFTENER LEVELS
- CLEAN INTERIOR AND EXTERIOR WINDOWS
- CHECK WINDOWS AND DOORS FOR AIR OR WATER LEAKS
- CHECK ROOF FOR LOOSE SHINGLES AND THAT VENTS ARE CLEAR
- TRIM LARGE TREES AND SHRUBS CLOSE TO THE HOUSE
- HAVE GAS HEATING SYSTEM INSPECTED
- REMOVE OR COVER EXTERIOR WINDOW AC UNITS
- CLEAN AND COVER OUTDOOR FURNITURE
- CHECK ATTIC FOR ANY DAYLIGHT COMING THROUGH THE ROOF INDICATING A LEAK/ HOLE

- HAVE FURNACE SERVICED
- OPEN WINDOWS ON WEATHER-PERMITTING DAYS TO AIR OUT HOUSE
- DRAIN AND WINTERIZE SPRINKLER SYSTEM
- CHECK ALL FAUCETS FOR LEAKS
- RAKE LEAVES
- CLEAN GUTTERS AND DOWNSPOUTS
- STOCK UP ON WINTER SUPPLIES (SHOVELS, ICE MELT, ETC.) AND RESTOCK EMERGENCY KITS FOR VEHICLES AND HOME
- CHECK CHIMNEY FOR BLOCKAGES AND HAVE IT CLEANED AND INSPECTED
- RESEED AND FERTILIZE LAWN
- CHECK HOME WALKWAYS AND RAILINGS
- DISCONNECT EXTERIOR HOSES AND STORE AND SHUT OFF EXTERIOR FAUCETS
- COMPLETE ANY EXTERIOR REPAIRS
- CLEAN DRYER VENTS

# SEASONAL HOME MAINTENANCE

## ——— CHECKLIST ———

### WINTER

- VACUUM AND CLEAN VENTS
- CHECK CARBON MONOXIDE, SMOKE DETECTORS, AND FIRE EXTINGUISHERS
- CLEAN RANGE HOOD FILTERS
- INSPECT AND CHANGE HVAC FILTERS
- CLEAN INTERIOR AND EXTERIOR WINDOWS
- CHECK WINDOWS AND DOORS FOR AIR OR WATER LEAKS
- REVERSE CEILING FAN DIRECTION
- DRAIN SEDIMENT FROM WATER HEATER
- LUBRICATE DOOR LOCKS
- VACUUM AND CLEAN VENTS
- CHECK ATTIC FOR ANY DAYLIGHT COMING THROUGH THE ROOF, INDICATING A LEAK/HOLE

- CHECK WATER TANK FOR CRACKS
- INSPECT INSULATION
- INSPECT HUMIDIFIERS
- STORE SEASONAL TOOLS (RAKE, SHOVEL, ETC.)
- STOCK UP ON WINTER SUPPLIES (ICE, MELT, SALT, ETC.) IF NEEDED
- INSPECT EMERGENCY KIT AND RESTOCK AS NEEDED
- SEAL ALL HOLES AND CRACKS AROUND EXTERIOR OF THE HOME
- CLEAN ANY DIRT, LEAVES, OR INSECTS FROM THE POOL AND PREP POOL FOR WINTER

# SEASONAL HOME MAINTENANCE

## CHECKLIST

### SPRING

- VACUUM AND CLEAN VENTS
- CHECK CARBON MONOXIDE, SMOKE DETECTORS, AND FIRE EXTINGUISHERS
- REPLACE FURNACE FILTER
- CHECK UNDER SINK FOR LEAKS
- CLEAN RANGE HOOD FILTERS
- INSPECT AND CHANGE HVAC FILTERS
- CHECK WATER SOFTENER SALT LEVELS
- CLEAN INTERIOR AND EXTERIOR WINDOWS
- CHECK WINDOWS AND DOORS FOR AIR OR WATER LEAKS
- CHECK ROOF FOR LOOSE SHINGLES AND THAT VENTS ARE CLEAR
- TRIM LARGE TREES AND SHRUBS CLOSE TO THE HOUSE
- HAVE AC SYSTEM INSPECTED
- REMOVE AND CLEAN OUTDOOR FURNITURE COVERS
- CLEAN OUTDOOR FURNITURE

- CHECK ATTIC FOR ANY DAYLIGHT COMING THROUGH THE ROOF, INDICATING A LEAK/HOLE
- REPLACE FURNACE FILTERS
- OPEN WINDOWS ON WEATHER-PERMITTING DAYS TO AIR OUT HOUSE
- CHECK HOME WALKWAYS AND RAILINGS
- CHECK ALL FAUCETS FOR LEAKS
- RAKE LEAVES
- CLEAN GUTTERS AND DOWNSPOUTS
- CONNECT EXTERIOR HOSES
- COMPLETE ANY EXTERIOR REPAIRS
- CLEAN DRYER VENTS
- CLEAN GRILL
- CHECK ROOF FOR WATER DAMAGE
- PRUNE AND CLEAN EXTERIOR FLOWER BEDS
- CLEAN EXTERIOR TRASH BINS

# SEASONAL HOME MAINTENANCE

## CHECKLIST

### SUMMER

- VACUUM AND CLEAN VENTS
- CLEAN GARBAGE DISPOSAL
- CHECK CARBON MONOXIDE, SMOKE DETECTORS, AND FIRE EXTINGUISHERS
- CLEAN RANGE HOOD FILTERS
- INSPECT AND CHANGE HVAC FILTERS
- CHECK WATER SOFTENER SALT LEVELS
- CLEAN INTERIOR AND EXTERIOR WINDOWS
- CHECK WINDOWS AND DOORS FOR AIR OR WATER LEAKS
- CLEAN BATHROOM DRAINS
- CLEAN AND REPLACE SHOWERHEADS
- REVERSE DIRECTION OF CEILING FANS
- INSPECT FENCE FOR NEEDED REPAIRS
- INSPECT MAILBOX FOR NEEDED REPAIRS

- CHECK ATTIC FOR ANY DAYLIGHT COMING THROUGH THE ROOF, INDICATING A LEAK/ HOLE
- OPEN WINDOWS ON WEATHER-PERMITTING DAYS TO AIR OUT HOUSE
- PRESSURE-WASH HOUSE EXTERIORS
- CLEAN PORCH
- WASH, CHANGE, OR REPAIR WINDOW SCREENS
- ADD MULCH TO LANDSCAPING
- CHECK FOR OUTDOOR LEAKS
- CHECK OUTDOOR PLAY EQUIPMENT
- DECLUTTER AND CLEAN OUTDOOR SHED
- INSPECT EXTERIOR DECK BOARDS AND RESEAL DECK IF NEEDED
- CLEAN EXTERIOR LIGHT FIXTURES
- CLEAN AND PREP POOL FOR THE SUMMER

# HOME MAINTENANCE

## CALENDAR

| JANUARY | FEBRUARY | MARCH |
|---|---|---|
| ☐ _____ | ☐ _____ | ☐ _____ |
| ☐ _____ | ☐ _____ | ☐ _____ |
| ☐ _____ | ☐ _____ | ☐ _____ |
| ☐ _____ | ☐ _____ | ☐ _____ |
| ☐ _____ | ☐ _____ | ☐ _____ |
| ☐ _____ | ☐ _____ | ☐ _____ |
| ☐ _____ | ☐ _____ | ☐ _____ |

| APRIL | MAY | JUNE |
|---|---|---|
| ☐ _____ | ☐ _____ | ☐ _____ |
| ☐ _____ | ☐ _____ | ☐ _____ |
| ☐ _____ | ☐ _____ | ☐ _____ |
| ☐ _____ | ☐ _____ | ☐ _____ |
| ☐ _____ | ☐ _____ | ☐ _____ |
| ☐ _____ | ☐ _____ | ☐ _____ |

# HOME MAINTENANCE

## CALENDAR

| JULY | AUGUST | SEPTEMBER |
|------|--------|-----------|
| ☐ _____ | ☐ _____ | ☐ _____ |
| ☐ _____ | ☐ _____ | ☐ _____ |
| ☐ _____ | ☐ _____ | ☐ _____ |
| ☐ _____ | ☐ _____ | ☐ _____ |
| ☐ _____ | ☐ _____ | ☐ _____ |
| ☐ _____ | ☐ _____ | ☐ _____ |
| ☐ _____ | ☐ _____ | ☐ _____ |

| OCTOBER | NOVEMBER | DECEMBER |
|---------|----------|----------|
| ☐ _____ | ☐ _____ | ☐ _____ |
| ☐ _____ | ☐ _____ | ☐ _____ |
| ☐ _____ | ☐ _____ | ☐ _____ |
| ☐ _____ | ☐ _____ | ☐ _____ |
| ☐ _____ | ☐ _____ | ☐ _____ |
| ☐ _____ | ☐ _____ | ☐ _____ |
| ☐ _____ | ☐ _____ | ☐ _____ |

# SERVICE PROVIDER

## LAWN & GARDEN PROFESSIONAL

| NAME | ADDRESS |
|---|---|
| PHONE | EMAIL |
| WEBSITE | |

## HANDYMAN

| NAME | ADDRESS |
|---|---|
| PHONE | EMAIL |
| WEBSITE | |

## ELECTRICIAN

| NAME | ADDRESS |
|---|---|
| PHONE | EMAIL |
| WEBSITE | |

## PAINTER

| NAME | ADDRESS |
|---|---|
| PHONE | EMAIL |
| WEBSITE | |

| PRESSURE WASHER | |
|---|---|
| NAME | ADDRESS |
| PHONE | EMAIL |
| WEBSITE | |

| PLUMBER | |
|---|---|
| NAME | ADDRESS |
| PHONE | EMAIL |
| WEBSITE | |

| CARPENTER | |
|---|---|
| NAME | ADDRESS |
| PHONE | EMAIL |
| WEBSITE | |

| VEHICLE MECHANIC | |
|---|---|
| NAME | ADDRESS |
| PHONE | EMAIL |
| WEBSITE | |

# HOME PROJECT SHEET

## TO-DO LIST

- _____
- _____
- _____
- _____

- _____
- _____
- _____
- _____

| ACTION | START DATE | COMPLETION DATE | COMPLETED BY | COMPLETE |
|--------|-----------|-----------------|--------------|----------|
|        |           |                 |              |          |
|        |           |                 |              |          |
|        |           |                 |              |          |
|        |           |                 |              |          |
|        |           |                 |              |          |
|        |           |                 |              |          |
|        |           |                 |              |          |
|        |           |                 |              |          |
|        |           |                 |              |          |
|        |           |                 |              |          |
|        |           |                 |              |          |
|        |           |                 |              |          |
|        |           |                 |              |          |
|        |           |                 |              |          |

# HOME PROJECT SHEET

## TO-DO LIST

- _____
- _____
- _____
- _____

- _____
- _____
- _____
- _____

| ACTION | START DATE | COMPLETION DATE | COMPLETED BY | COMPLETE |
|--------|-----------|-----------------|--------------|----------|
|        |           |                 |              |          |
|        |           |                 |              |          |
|        |           |                 |              |          |
|        |           |                 |              |          |
|        |           |                 |              |          |
|        |           |                 |              |          |
|        |           |                 |              |          |
|        |           |                 |              |          |
|        |           |                 |              |          |
|        |           |                 |              |          |
|        |           |                 |              |          |
|        |           |                 |              |          |
|        |           |                 |              |          |
|        |           |                 |              |          |

# PAINT COLOR TRACKER

## LOCATION _____

DATE LAST PAINTED _____

PAINT BRAND _____

PAINT COLOR _____

PAINT NUMBER _____

QTY. NEEDED FOR AREA _____

PAINT

CHIP

HERE

## LOCATION _____

DATE LAST PAINTED _____

PAINT BRAND _____

PAINT COLOR _____

PAINT NUMBER _____

QTY. NEEDED FOR AREA _____

PAINT

CHIP

HERE

## LOCATION _____

DATE LAST PAINTED _____

PAINT BRAND _____

PAINT COLOR _____

PAINT NUMBER _____

QTY. NEEDED FOR AREA _____

PAINT

CHIP

HERE

# PAINT COLOR TRACKER

## LOCATION _____

DATE LAST PAINTED _____

PAINT BRAND _____

PAINT COLOR _____

PAINT NUMBER _____

QTY. NEEDED FOR AREA _____

PAINT

CHIP

HERE

## LOCATION _____

DATE LAST PAINTED _____

PAINT BRAND _____

PAINT COLOR _____

PAINT NUMBER _____

QTY. NEEDED FOR AREA _____

PAINT

CHIP

HERE

## LOCATION _____

DATE LAST PAINTED _____

PAINT BRAND _____

PAINT COLOR _____

PAINT NUMBER _____

QTY. NEEDED FOR AREA _____

PAINT

CHIP

HERE

# PAINT COLOR TRACKER

## LOCATION _____

DATE LAST PAINTED _____

PAINT BRAND _____

PAINT COLOR _____

PAINT NUMBER _____

QTY. NEEDED FOR AREA _____

PAINT
CHIP
HERE

## LOCATION _____

DATE LAST PAINTED _____

PAINT BRAND _____

PAINT COLOR _____

PAINT NUMBER _____

QTY. NEEDED FOR AREA _____

PAINT
CHIP
HERE

## LOCATION _____

DATE LAST PAINTED _____

PAINT BRAND _____

PAINT COLOR _____

PAINT NUMBER _____

QTY. NEEDED FOR AREA _____

PAINT
CHIP
HERE

# PAINT COLOR TRACKER

## LOCATION _____

DATE LAST PAINTED _____

PAINT BRAND _____

PAINT COLOR _____

PAINT NUMBER _____

QTY. NEEDED FOR AREA _____

PAINT CHIP HERE

## LOCATION _____

DATE LAST PAINTED _____

PAINT BRAND _____

PAINT COLOR _____

PAINT NUMBER _____

QTY. NEEDED FOR AREA _____

PAINT CHIP HERE

## LOCATION _____

DATE LAST PAINTED _____

PAINT BRAND _____

PAINT COLOR _____

PAINT NUMBER _____

QTY. NEEDED FOR AREA _____

PAINT CHIP HERE

# PAINT COLOR TRACKER

## INTERIOR

### LOCATION _____

DATE LAST PAINTED _____

PAINT BRAND _____

PAINT COLOR _____

PAINT NUMBER _____

QTY. NEEDED FOR AREA _____

PAINT

CHIP

HERE

### LOCATION _____

DATE LAST PAINTED _____

PAINT BRAND _____

PAINT COLOR _____

PAINT NUMBER _____

QTY. NEEDED FOR AREA _____

PAINT

CHIP

HERE

### LOCATION _____

DATE LAST PAINTED _____

PAINT BRAND _____

PAINT COLOR _____

PAINT NUMBER _____

QTY. NEEDED FOR AREA _____

PAINT

CHIP

HERE

# HOME HISTORY LOG

| ITEM | DATE PURCHASED | APPROXIMATE REPLACEMENT DATE |
|---|---|---|
| ROOF | | |
| CAULKING | | |
| WOOD DECKING | | |
| DOORS | | |
| FOUNDATION | | |
| GARAGE DOOR OPENERS | | |
| PAINTS AND STAINS | | |
| SHUTTERS | | |
| SIDING / BRICK | | |
| WINDOWS | | |
| FRIDGE | | |
| FREEZER | | |
| STOVE | | |
| OVEN | | |
| DISHWASHER | | |
| GARBAGE DISPOSAL | | |
| WASHING MACHINE | | |
| DRYER | | |
| VACUUM | | |
| CARPET SHAMPOOER | | |

# HOME HISTORY LOG

| WARRANTY | WARRANTY EXPIRATION | NOTES |
|----------|---------------------|-------|
| Y / N | | |
| Y / N | | |
| Y / N | | |
| Y / N | | |
| Y / N | | |
| Y / N | | |
| Y / N | | |
| Y / N | | |
| Y / N | | |
| Y / N | | |
| Y / N | | |
| Y / N | | |
| Y / N | | |
| Y / N | | |
| Y / N | | |
| Y / N | | |
| Y / N | | |
| Y / N | | |
| Y / N | | |
| Y / N | | |

# HOME HISTORY LOG

| ITEM | DATE PURCHASED | APPROXIMATE REPLACEMENT DATE |
|------|----------------|------------------------------|
| MASTER BR MATTRESS | | |
| _____ BR MATTRESS | | |
| _____ BR MATTRESS | | |
| _____ BR MATTRESS | | |
| _____ BR MATTRESS | | |
| _____ BR MATTRESS | | |
| CARPET | | |
| HARD FLOORING | | |
| LAWN MOWER | | |
| GRILL | | |
| COMPUTER _____ | | |
| COMPUTER _____ | | |
| COMPUTER _____ | | |
| COMPUTER _____ | | |
| COMPUTER _____ | | |
| TELEVISION _____ | | |
| TELEVISION _____ | | |
| TELEVISION _____ | | |
| TELEVISION _____ | | |
| TELEVISION _____ | | |

# HOME HISTORY LOG

| WARRANTY | WARRANTY EXPIRATION | NOTES |
| --- | --- | --- |
| Y / N | | |
| Y / N | | |
| Y / N | | |
| Y / N | | |
| Y / N | | |
| Y / N | | |
| Y / N | | |
| Y / N | | |
| Y / N | | |
| Y / N | | |
| Y / N | | |
| Y / N | | |
| Y / N | | |
| Y / N | | |
| Y / N | | |
| Y / N | | |
| Y / N | | |
| Y / N | | |
| Y / N | | |
| Y / N | | |

# HOME HISTORY LOG

| ITEM | DATE PURCHASED | APPROXIMATE REPLACEMENT DATE |
|------|----------------|------------------------------|
| AUTOMOBILE _____ | | |
| AUTOMOBILE _____ | | |
| AUTOMOBILE _____ | | |
| AUTOMOBILE _____ | | |
| OTHER _____ | | |
| OTHER _____ | | |
| OTHER _____ | | |
| OTHER _____ | | |
| OTHER _____ | | |
| OTHER _____ | | |
| OTHER _____ | | |
| OTHER _____ | | |
| OTHER _____ | | |
| OTHER _____ | | |
| OTHER _____ | | |
| OTHER _____ | | |
| OTHER _____ | | |
| OTHER _____ | | |
| OTHER _____ | | |
| OTHER _____ | | |

# HOME HISTORY LOG

| WARRANTY | WARRANTY EXPIRATION | NOTES |
|---|---|---|
| Y / N | | |
| Y / N | | |
| Y / N | | |
| Y / N | | |
| Y / N | | |
| Y / N | | |
| Y / N | | |
| Y / N | | |
| Y / N | | |
| Y / N | | |
| Y / N | | |
| Y / N | | |
| Y / N | | |
| Y / N | | |
| Y / N | | |
| Y / N | | |
| Y / N | | |
| Y / N | | |
| Y / N | | |
| Y / N | | |

# VEHICLE MAINTENANCE LOG

| VEHICLE MAKE | | VEHICLE MODEL | | VEHICLE COLOR | | | YEAR |
|---|---|---|---|---|---|---|---|
| | | | | | | | |

| TYPE OF SERVICE | DATE | DATE | DATE | DATE | DATE | DATE |
|---|---|---|---|---|---|---|
| OIL CHANGE (SEE AUTO MANUAL) | | | | | | |
| MILEAGE | | | | | | |
| TRANSMISSION FLUID (EVERY 20,000 MILES) | | | | | | |
| MILEAGE | | | | | | |
| COOLANT (EVERY 6 MONTHS) | | | | | | |
| MILEAGE | | | | | | |
| BELTS & HOSES (EVERY 50,000 MILES) | | | | | | |
| MILEAGE | | | | | | |
| BATTERY CHECK (EVERY 6 MONTHS) | | | | | | |
| MILEAGE | | | | | | |
| ROTATE/BALANCE TIRES (EVERY 7000 MILES) | | | | | | |
| MILEAGE | | | | | | |
| SPARK PLUGS (EVERY 30,000 MILES) | | | | | | |
| MILEAGE | | | | | | |
| REPLACE TIRES (SEE AUTO MANUAL) | | | | | | |
| MILEAGE | | | | | | |
| ALIGNMENT (EVERY 30,000 MILES) | | | | | | |
| MILEAGE | | | | | | |
| CHECK BRAKES (EVERY 10,000 MILES) | | | | | | |
| MILEAGE | | | | | | |
| REPLACE FILTERS (EVERY 15,000 MILES) | | | | | | |
| MILEAGE | | | | | | |
| WIPER BLADES (EVERY 6 MONTHS) | | | | | | |
| MILEAGE | | | | | | |
| CHECK SUSPENSION (EVERY 50,000 MILES) | | | | | | |
| MILEAGE | | | | | | |
| SERVICE AIR CONDITIONER (EVERY 2 YEARS) | | | | | | |
| MILEAGE | | | | | | |

# ESSENTIAL № 4

# HOME CLEANING

If there's one thing about home management that's easy to put off, it's cleaning! Cleaning the house can feel daunting and repetitive. But having systems in place and a routine that involves the whole family makes it much easier. Of course you'll need to tailor your routine based on the size of your family, the design of your home, and your lifestyle, but this chapter can act as a guide to help you keep up with cleaning and avoid the stress of a mess.

## CREATE FAMILY BUY-IN

Creating family buy-in to keep your home tidy is the secret weapon to cleaning success in your home. When one family member is pulling the load of completing chores around the home alone, it can often cause resentment and tension between family members. This is why it is essential to keep up with consistent family meetings, to keep communication strong and share expectations for keeping the home tidy. Having the entire family share in the responsibilities of the home is important for these reasons:

- FOSTERS TEAMWORK AND BUILDS FAMILY UNITY
- TEACHES YOUNGER FAMILY MEMBERS LIFE SKILLS
- MINIMIZES THE STRESS IN THE HOME
- HELPS MAINTAIN A TIDY HOME

## CLEANING ROUTINES

There is a variety of cleaning routines you can incorporate to maintain your home. Depending on the activity that goes on in your home, you may need to incorporate each of the following routines, or you may only need one of them. Again, we all live differently in our spaces, so it's important to understand the unique needs of your home and family.

## DAILY

Spending twenty minutes a day cleaning your home is an excellent way to stay on top of things. This basically entails cleaning up behind yourself and your family. If you don't tackle some cleaning each day, then it may potentially impact your home and family negatively. Use the Daily Cleaning Routine (page 76) to help your family create a plan for what to clean from one day to the next.

## WEEKLY

Weekly cleaning is a great opportunity to dedicate a few hours a week to completely clean your home. It can take about a week for a home to become quite messy, if unattended to, so weekly cleanings are at that boundary level of "must" do. Use the Weekly Cleaning Routine (pages 77-78) as a checklist.

## MONTHLY

For a monthly cleaning routine, simply identify when you will do each cleaning task in your home throughout the month. Establishing this kind of routine gives you a monthly view of cleaning your home, and it can be quite easy to maintain once the family is on board. The annual cleaning routine can be implemented in your home to rotate tasks as appropriate. Use the Monthly Cleaning Routine (pages 79-80) as a checklist for cleaning your home.

## SPRING CLEANING

Annual cleaning routines are what we call "spring cleaning." This is the process of giving your home a deep cleaning from top to bottom. This is definitely a task that you do not want to take on alone unless necessary—get your other family members involved. One great tool to use is a spring-cleaning box. This is a fun way to incorporate the family into the process of spring cleaning the home.

## THE SPRING CLEANING BOX

Using the Spring Cleaning Box Guide (pages 84-85), create index cards for each item/task and put them all in a box, organized or color-coded by room. Then place the box in your entryway. The family goal is to complete all of the cards within a two-week window. Have people draw a few cards each day and see how fast you can empty the box. At the end of the spring-cleaning season, the family member with the most completed cards receives a reward. The spring-cleaning box takes a massive cleaning task and makes it a fun, interactive game the whole family will enjoy.

# DAILY CLEANING ROUTINE

YOU AND YOUR FAMILY WILL AGREE ON THE CLEANING TASKS YOU ARE
EXPECTED TO DO EACH DAY.

- MAKE BEDS
- EMPTY DISHES (A.M.)
- DO YOUR DISHES AS YOU USE THEM
  THROUGHOUT THE DAY
- LOAD DISHWASHER (P.M.)
- SORT MAIL
- CLEAN UP TOYS AFTER PLAYTIME
- QUICK ORGANIZATION TASK*
- AS NEEDED*
- NIGHT ROUTINE*

| QUICK ORGANIZATION TASK | Find one small area of the home (kitchen drawers, linen closet, toy bin) and spend 5-10 minutes organizing. |
|---|---|
| AS NEEDED | To do throughout the week as needed: load laundry, fold and put away laundry, sweep up floors and messes. |
| NIGHT ROUTINE | General pickup of items around the home, wipe-down of kitchen (including appliances), take out trash, and sanitize home by disinfecting doorknobs, kitchen and bath handles, etc. |

# WEEKLY CLEANING ROUTINE

## CHECKLIST

### KITCHEN

- WASH DISHES AND CLEAN STOVETOP AND BURNERS
- CLEAN COUNTERS
- WIPE DOWN APPLIANCES
- CLEAN OUT FRIDGE
- CLEAN FLOORS

### LIVING AREAS

- OPEN WINDOWS
- SPOT CLEAN FURNITURE
- CLEAN LAMPS AND LAMPSHADES
- DUST LIGHT FIXTURES AND SURFACES
- VACUUM FURNITURE AND CLEAN FLOORS

# WEEKLY CLEANING ROUTINE

## CHECKLIST

### BATHROOMS

- WASH OUTSIDE OF CABINETS AND VANITIES
- DUST LIGHT FIXTURES
- WIPE DOWN MIRRORS
- WIPE DOWN AND SANITIZE COUNTERS AND SINKS
- CLEAN TUB AND DRAIN
- CLEAN TOILET (INSIDE AND OUTSIDE)
- WIPE DOWN DOORS, KNOBS, SWITCHES, TRIM, AND BASEBOARDS

### BEDROOMS

- TIDY AND ORGANIZE DRESSER DRAWERS
- TIDY AND ORGANIZE CLOSET
- WASH SHEETS, PILLOW CASES AND DUVET COVERS
- AIR OUT MATTRESS PADS
- WIPE DOWN DOORS, KNOBS, SWITCHES, TRIM, AND BASEBOARDS
- WASH WINDOWS AND WINDOWSILLS
- DUST LIGHT FIXTURES AND SURFACES
- VACUUM FLOORS

### OUTDOORS

- WASH THRESHOLDS
- SWEEP PORCHES, PATIOS, AND WALKWAYS
- CLEAN DOORMATS

# MONTHLY CLEANING ROUTINE

## CHECKLIST

### KITCHEN

- CLEAN MICROWAVE
- CLEAN COFFEE MAKER
- WIPE REFRIGERATOR SHELVES
- DECLUTTER CONDIMENTS
- CLEAN OUT ONE REFRIGERATOR DRAWERS
- WIPE OUT SILVERWARE DRAWER
- SCRUB SINK
- CLEAN DISHWASHER
- CLEAN TOASTER
- DECLUTTER COOKBOOKS
- TOSS RECIPES YOU NO LONGER LOVE

### BATHROOM

- CLEAN THE TOILET (DOWN TO THE FLOOR)
- EMPTY AND WIPE OUT A DRAWER
- ORGANIZE PRODUCTS AND MAKEUP
- WASH SHOWER CURTAIN
- CLEAN BASEBOARDS

### BEDROOMS

- WASH MATTRESS PADS
- FLUFF COMFORTER IN DRYER
- CLEAN PILLOWS
- ORGANIZE AND CLEAN NIGHTSTAND
- DUST LAMPSHADES
- VACUUM UNDER BED

### CLOSETS & DRAWERS

- PULL ITEMS TO DONATE
- WIPE DOWN SHELVES
- ORGANIZE CLOTHES BY TYPE (SHIRTS, PANTS, ETC.)
- TOSS ANY UNMATCHED SOCKS

### LAUNDRY ROOM

- WIPE DOWN WASHER AND DRYER EXTERIORS
- CLEAN AND AIR-DRY LINT TRAP

# MONTHLY CLEANING ROUTINE

## CHECKLIST

### ELECTRONICS

- WIPE DOWN CELL PHONES
- WIPE DOWN LANDLINE PHONES
- CLEAN TV AND COMPUTER SCREENS
- WIPE DOWN REMOTES
- WIPE DOWN COMPUTER MOUSES

### VEHICLES

- COLLECT ANY TRASH FROM CAR AND TOSS
- DUST/VACUUM FRONT INTERIOR OF VEHICLE
- WIPE BEVERAGE HOLDERS
- CLEAN UNDER SEATS

### PAPER

- GO THROUGH MAGAZINES AND RECYCLE
- TACKLE YOUR PAPER PILE
- CLEAN OUT YOUR WALLET OR PURSE
- FILE ANY RECEIPTS

### OUTDOORS

- POWER-WASH SIDING AND DRIVEWAY

### OTHER

- _____
- _____
- _____
- _____
- _____
- _____
- _____
- _____
- _____
- _____
- _____
- _____
- _____
- _____

# BASIC TO-DO LIST

WEEK OF:

WEEK OF:

# BASIC TO-DO LIST

**WEEK OF:**

- _____
- _____
- _____
- _____
- _____
- _____
- _____
- _____
- _____
- _____
- _____
- _____
- _____
- _____
- _____
- _____
- _____
- _____
- _____
- _____
- _____
- _____

**WEEK OF:**

- _____
- _____
- _____
- _____
- _____
- _____
- _____
- _____
- _____
- _____
- _____
- _____
- _____
- _____
- _____
- _____
- _____
- _____
- _____
- _____
- _____
- _____

# LAUNDRY SYMBOL GUIDE

**MACHINE WASH NORMAL**

**MACHINE WASH COLD**

**MACHINE WASH WARM**

**MACHINE WASH HOT 50°C / 120 °F**

**MACHINE WASH HOT 60°C / 140 °F**

**MACHINE WASH HOT 70°C / 180 °F**

**MACHINE WASH HOT 90°C / 200 °F**

**MACHINE WASH PERMANENT PRESS**

**MACHINE WASH GENTLE**

**HAND WASH NORMAL**

**BLEACH WHEN NEEDED**

**NON-CHLORINE BLEACH WHEN NEEDED**

**DO NOT BLEACH**

**DRY CLEAN**

**DO NOT DRY CLEAN**

**DRY**

**DO NOT DRY**

**DO NOT TUMBLE DRY**

**DRY FLAT**

**DRY IN THE SHADE**

**HANG TO DRY**

**DRIP DRY**

**TUMBLE DRY NORMAL NO HEAT**

**DO NOT WRING**

**TUMBLE DRY NORMAL**

**TUMBLE DRY NORMAL LOW HEAT**

**TUMBLE DRY NORMAL MEDIUM HEAT**

**TUMBLE DRY NORMAL HIGH HEAT**

**TUMBLE DRY PERMANENT PRESS**

**TUMBLE DRY GENTLE NO HEAT**

**IRON ANY TEMPERATURE STEAM OR DRY**

**IRON LOW HEAT**

**IRON MEDIUM HEAT**

**IRON HIGH HEAT**

**DO NOT IRON**

**DO NOT STEAM**

# SPRING CLEANING BOX GUIDE

HERE ARE SOME IDEAS FOR WHAT TO PUT IN A SPRING CLEANING BOX. CUSTOMIZE THE CATEGORIES AND CARDS TO FIT YOUR ANNUAL CLEANING NEEDS.

### FOYER

Clean windows

Clean front door

Clean light fixture

Clean switch plates

Wash walls

### OFFICE

Clean windows

Purge desk

Purge files

Clean draperies

Clean switch plates

Wash walls

### DINING ROOM

Clean light fixture

Clean switch plates

Clean windows

Clean draperies

Clean & purge china cabinet

Wash walls

### LIVING ROOM

Clean light fixture

Clean switch plates

Clean windows

Clean draperies

Clean and purge cabinets

Wash walls

### KITCHEN

Clean oven

Clean behind fridge

Clean & purge pantry

Clean & purge cabinets

Clean draperies

Deep clean appliances

Wash walls & cabinets

Clean windows & doors

### LAUNDRY ROOM

Clean behind washer & dryer

Purge & organize cabinets

Wash walls

# SPRING CLEANING BOX GUIDE

### BEDROOMS

Clean windows

Clean doors

Clean light fixture

Clean switch plates

Clean upholstery

Clean draperies & linens

Wash walls

### BATHROOMS

Clean windows

Clean doors

Clean light fixture

Clean switch plates

Clean upholstery

Wash walls

Clean drains

Replace old towels

Purge & clean cabinets

### DEN

Clean electronics

Wash walls

Clean lights & switch plates

Clean doors

## EXTERIOR

### GARAGE

Clean large equipment & tools

Purge excess items

Clean light fixtures

Clean switch plates

Clean floors

Clean windows

Clean garage doors

### AUTOMOBILE

Clean exterior

Clean interior

Clean carpets

Organize car documents

### MISC.

Get air conditioner serviced

Complete fire safety checks

Purge medicine cabinet

Purge & organize linen closet

Purge & clean attic

Clean carpets

# ESSENTIAL №5

# PARENT-SCHOOL SYSTEM

*IF YOU DON'T HAVE SCHOOL-AGED CHILDREN, FEEL FREE TO SKIP TO CHAPTER 7

One thing that can quickly fill up a family calendar is school and extracurricular activities. Between field trips, soccer practice, and PTA meetings, it can be a full-time job coordinating the family schedules and school responsibilities. This makes it especially important to have an efficient system in place to prevent you from feeling like you are a hamster in a wheel.

Parents tend to kick into survival mode when the school year starts. It can be challenging to keep track of how your child is doing in school and what's coming up next when the lunch money is due, when the annual school fundraiser kicks off, when permission slips are due—the list goes on! That's why it's extremely handy to have a resource that makes you a rock-star parent who is on top of your game. How do you do this? By creating a parent-school binder. This is such an essential home tool to make sure that you, as parents, know exactly what is going on with your child—in a way that does not consume a lot of your valuable time.

## CREATING A PARENT-SCHOOL BINDER

The first thing to understand about creating a parent-school binder is that this binder is for the parent, not the student. Your child doesn't need access to this binder. To get started, gather the following items:

- **THREE-RING BINDER:** When choosing a binder, pick something that is in your favorite color or features a pattern you love. Have fun and make it your masterpiece, because it is going to serve you for the entire school year.

- **POCKET FOLDERS:** You need a pocket folder for every school-age child in your home. Coordinate these pocket folders with your three-ring binder to make it beautiful. You can even color-code the pocket folders and identify each child by a different color. Choose pocket folders that are three-hole–punched so they fit in the three-ring binder.

- **BINDER PENCIL POUCH:** Select a binder pencil pouch for your binder. This pouch will be essential for keeping things like lunch money, tickets, and things of that nature.

Now that you have the three key components you need to create your parent-teacher binder, let's get started!

## ACADEMIC CALENDAR

The academic calendar is something that you want to be able to see as soon as you open your parent-school binder. This is basically going to be your brain when it comes to your child's education and activities. The dates that you want to keep on this calendar include:

- NO-SCHOOL DAYS
- PARENT/TEACHER CONFERENCE DATES
- EXTRACURRICULAR ACTIVITY APPOINTMENTS
- LUNCH AND TUITION PAYMENT DUE DATES
- REPORT CARD DATES
- SCHOOL TESTING DATES
- PTA MEETING DATES
- TEACHERS' BIRTHDAYS

In addition to documenting essential dates on your calendar, you can use it to track your children individually. Parents hear a variety of things during the course of the school year, such as, "I don't have homework today," or "I don't feel well. I don't want to go to school." This calendar can help you document trends. Each time your child comes home, take a minute to note a quick assessment of their day on the calendar. This will give you an overview of behavior and can help you identify if you need to address an ongoing or recurring issue.

You may think that having your own calendar is pointless if the school provides one. But the purpose of your calendar is to keep all of your kids' school information on one consolidated calendar, rather than having to shift between multiple calendars. Use the Academic Calendar (page 91) template to keep all of this essential information in one place. Copy the form and switch it out each month.

## ACTIVITY TRACKER

If your child participates in any other activities, keep a separate log of practices, instructor info, payments, and equipment, etc. Use the Extracurricular Activity Tracker worksheet (page 92) to keep track of this information. Make copies depending on how many children you have and their activities!

## LUNCH MENU/LUNCH PLAN

Keep a copy of the current lunch menu in your parent-school binder so that you can easily see if there are dates when your child may need to take their own lunch because of food sensitivities or allergies. This is the perfect tool to have at your fingertips to be aware of what your child is scheduled to eat each day. If your child takes their lunch to school, it's a great idea to plan out their menus for the month. This cuts down on the stress of planning this every day. Use the Lunch Planner guide (page 93) to plan your child's lunches.

## SCHOOL INFORMATION SHEET

The School Information Sheet (pages 94-97) gives you an overview of everything as it relates to your child's school and classes. This handy sheet keeps things right at your fingertips and makes it simple when you need to follow up with teachers.

## AFTER-SCHOOL ROUTINE

Use the After-School Routine Flowchart (page 99) to guide each child's daily routine when they get home from school. You can use the sample (page 98) as a reference.

## PLEASE-EXCUSE NOTES

Being prepared to notify your child's school when you need to check your child out of school early or change their transportation source, or even when they are out sick, can be simplified by keeping "Excuse Notes" handy in your parent-school binder. The Please Excuse Notes template (page 100) makes sending excuse notes to school with your child easy and convenient.

## BACK-TO-SCHOOL CHECKLIST

The weeks leading up to the start of the school year can be very busy. Use the handy Back-to-School Checklist (pages 101-105) to make sure you don't forget anything as you and your family prepare for the kids to go back to school.

# ACADEMIC CALENDAR

MONTH OF ————————————

| SUNDAY | MONDAY | TUESDAY | WEDNESDAY | THURSDAY | FRIDAY | SATURDAY |
|--------|--------|---------|-----------|----------|--------|----------|
|        |        |         |           |          |        |          |
|        |        |         |           |          |        |          |
|        |        |         |           |          |        |          |
|        |        |         |           |          |        |          |
|        |        |         |           |          |        |          |

NOTES

_____

_____

_____

# EXTRACURRICULAR

## ACTIVITY TRACKER

| | | | |
|---|---|---|---|
| **CHILD** | | | |
| **ACTIVITY** | | | |
| **LOCATION** | | | |
| **DAY(S)** | | | |
| **INSTRUCTOR** | | | |
| **CONTACT NUMBER** | | | |
| **CONTACT EMAIL** | | | |
| **COST** | | | |

| PAYMENTS | | | |
|---|---|---|---|
| **DUE DATE** | **AMOUNT** | **DATE PAID** | **NOTES** |
| | | | |
| | | | |
| | | | |
| | | | |
| | | | |
| | | | |

| EQUIPMENT / SUPPLIES / UNIFORMS | | | |
|---|---|---|---|
| **ITEM** | **COST** | **DATE PURCHASED** | **NOTES** |
| | | | |
| | | | |
| | | | |
| | | | |
| | | | |
| | | | |

# LUNCH PLANNER

| | MONDAY | TUESDAY | WEDNESDAY | THURSDAY | FRIDAY |
|---|---|---|---|---|---|
| **MORNING SNACK** | | | | | |
| **LUNCH** | | | | | |
| **AFTERNOON SNACK** | | | | | |

## SHOPPING LIST

- _____
- _____
- _____
- _____
- _____
- _____
- _____
- _____
- _____

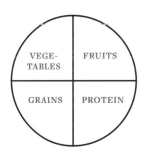

| WEEKLY BUDGET | $ |
|---|---|
| TOTAL AMOUNT SPENT | $ |

# SCHOOL INFORMATION

| NAME | | SCHOOL ADDRESS | |
|------|---|----------------|---|
| GRADE | | SCHOOL TELEPHONE | |
| SCHOOL | | SCHOOL WEBSITE | |

| TEACHER | SUBJECT | PERIOD | EMAIL | TELEPHONE |
|---------|---------|--------|-------|-----------|
| | | | | |
| | | | | |
| | | | | |
| | | | | |
| | | | | |
| | | | | |
| | | | | |

| NAME | | SCHOOL ADDRESS | |
|------|---|----------------|---|
| GRADE | | SCHOOL TELEPHONE | |
| SCHOOL | | SCHOOL WEBSITE | |

| TEACHER | SUBJECT | PERIOD | EMAIL | TELEPHONE |
|---------|---------|--------|-------|-----------|
| | | | | |
| | | | | |
| | | | | |
| | | | | |
| | | | | |
| | | | | |
| | | | | |

# SCHOOL INFORMATION

| NAME | | SCHOOL ADDRESS | |
|---|---|---|---|
| GRADE | | SCHOOL TELEPHONE | |
| SCHOOL | | SCHOOL WEBSITE | |

| TEACHER | SUBJECT | PERIOD | EMAIL | TELEPHONE |
|---|---|---|---|---|
| | | | | |
| | | | | |
| | | | | |
| | | | | |
| | | | | |
| | | | | |
| | | | | |

| NAME | | SCHOOL ADDRESS | |
|---|---|---|---|
| GRADE | | SCHOOL TELEPHONE | |
| SCHOOL | | SCHOOL WEBSITE | |

| TEACHER | SUBJECT | PERIOD | EMAIL | TELEPHONE |
|---|---|---|---|---|
| | | | | |
| | | | | |
| | | | | |
| | | | | |
| | | | | |
| | | | | |
| | | | | |

# SCHOOL INFORMATION

| | | | |
|---|---|---|---|
| NAME | | SCHOOL ADDRESS | |
| GRADE | | SCHOOL TELEPHONE | |
| SCHOOL | | SCHOOL WEBSITE | |

| TEACHER | SUBJECT | PERIOD | EMAIL | TELEPHONE |
|---|---|---|---|---|
| | | | | |
| | | | | |
| | | | | |
| | | | | |
| | | | | |
| | | | | |
| | | | | |

| | | | |
|---|---|---|---|
| NAME | | SCHOOL ADDRESS | |
| GRADE | | SCHOOL TELEPHONE | |
| SCHOOL | | SCHOOL WEBSITE | |

| TEACHER | SUBJECT | PERIOD | EMAIL | TELEPHONE |
|---|---|---|---|---|
| | | | | |
| | | | | |
| | | | | |
| | | | | |
| | | | | |
| | | | | |
| | | | | |

# SCHOOL INFORMATION

| NAME | | SCHOOL ADDRESS | |
|------|------|------|------|
| GRADE | | SCHOOL TELEPHONE | |
| SCHOOL | | SCHOOL WEBSITE | |

| TEACHER | SUBJECT | PERIOD | EMAIL | TELEPHONE |
|---------|---------|--------|-------|-----------|
| | | | | |
| | | | | |
| | | | | |
| | | | | |
| | | | | |
| | | | | |
| | | | | |

| NAME | | SCHOOL ADDRESS | |
|------|------|------|------|
| GRADE | | SCHOOL TELEPHONE | |
| SCHOOL | | SCHOOL WEBSITE | |

| TEACHER | SUBJECT | PERIOD | EMAIL | TELEPHONE |
|---------|---------|--------|-------|-----------|
| | | | | |
| | | | | |
| | | | | |
| | | | | |
| | | | | |
| | | | | |
| | | | | |

UNPACK BACKPACK.

NEED ANYTHING SIGNED BY PARENT? PLACE ON THE KITCHEN TABLE.

CHANGE OUT OF SCHOOL CLOTHES.

HAVE A SNACK.

COMPLETE HOMEWORK.

UNPACK AND PLACE BACKPACK BY THE DOOR.

COMPLETE CHORES.

GET SCHOOL CLOTHES READY FOR NEXT DAY.

FREE TIME.

## ROUTINE FLOWCHART

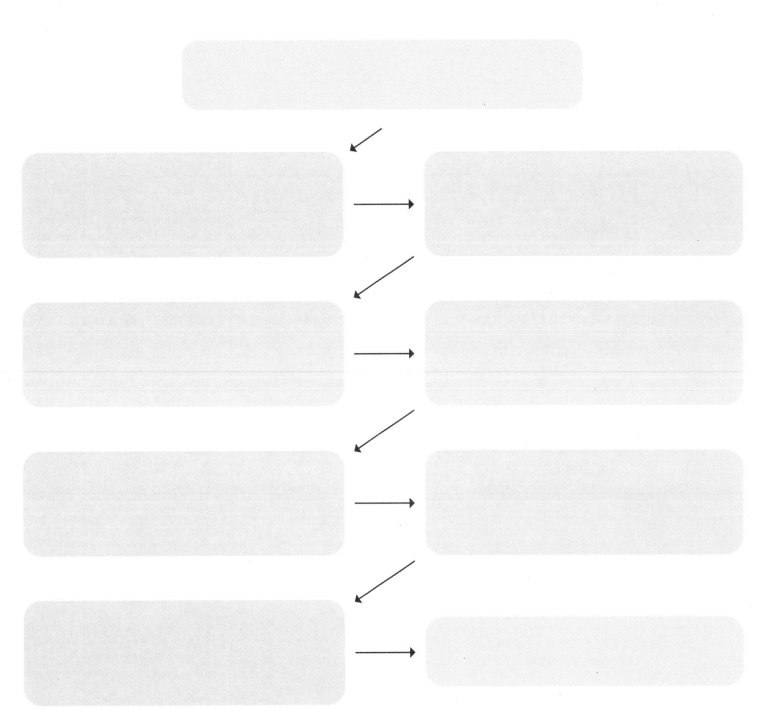

# PLEASE EXCUSE

_____

STUDENT

## FOR

● TARDY          ● ABSENT          ● OTHER _____

| ILLNESS | FAMILY MATTER |
|---------|---------------|
| DOCTOR | INJURY |
| DENTIST | OTHER |

● WILL BE LEAVING EARLY

TIME: _____

○ A.M.     REASON:

○ P.M.     _____

_____

● TRANSPORTATION CHANGE

BUS: _____

CAR RIDE WITH: _____

● OTHER _____

_____

PARENT SIGNATURE

PLEASE CONTACT ME IF YOU HAVE ANY QUESTIONS

TELEPHONE _____ EMAIL _____

# BACK-TO-SCHOOL

## REGISTRATION

| STUDENT | | | | |
|---|---|---|---|---|
| BIRTH CERTIFICATE | | | | |
| IMMUNIZATION RECORDS | | | | |
| SOCIAL SECURITY CARD | | | | |
| LEGAL PAPERWORK | | | | |
| HEALTH INFORMATION | | | | |
| PROOF OF RESIDENCY | | | | |
| EMERGENCY CONTACTS | | | | |
| IEP RECORDS | | | | |
| FORMER SCHOOL RECORDS | | | | |
| | | | | |
| | | | | |
| | | | | |
| | | | | |
| | | | | |
| | | | | |
| | | | | |

## CLOTHING, SHOES, AND ACCESSORIES

| STUDENT | | | | |
|---|---|---|---|---|
| PANTS / SKIRTS | | | | |
| TOPS | | | | |
| SWEATERS | | | | |
| WINTER COAT | | | | |
| RAINCOAT | | | | |
| JACKET | | | | |
| SHOES | | | | |
| SOCKS | | | | |
| UNDERWEAR | | | | |
| | | | | |
| | | | | |
| | | | | |
| | | | | |
| | | | | |
| | | | | |
| | | | | |
| | | | | |

# BACK-TO-SCHOOL

## CHECKLIST

### SUPPLIES

| STUDENT | | | | |
|---|---|---|---|---|
| BACKPACK / BOOK BAG | | | | |
| LUNCH BOX / BAG | | | | |
| HOMEWORK CADDY | | | | |
| PENCILS | | | | |
| PENCIL SHARPENER | | | | |
| PENS | | | | |
| BINDERS | | | | |
| BINDER DIVIDERS | | | | |
| FOLDERS | | | | |
| NOTEBOOKS | | | | |
| TISSUE | | | | |
| HAND SANITIZER | | | | |
| | | | | |
| | | | | |
| | | | | |
| | | | | |
| | | | | |

# BACK-TO-SCHOOL

## CHECKLIST

### SUPPLIES

| STUDENT | | | | |
|---|---|---|---|---|
| | | | | |
| | | | | |
| | | | | |
| | | | | |
| | | | | |
| | | | | |
| | | | | |
| | | | | |
| | | | | |
| | | | | |
| | | | | |
| | | | | |
| | | | | |
| | | | | |
| | | | | |
| | | | | |
| | | | | |
| | | | | |

# BACK-TO-SCHOOL

## CHECKLIST

### SUPPLIES

| STUDENT | | | | |
|---|---|---|---|---|
| | | | | |
| | | | | |
| | | | | |
| | | | | |
| | | | | |
| | | | | |
| | | | | |
| | | | | |
| | | | | |
| | | | | |
| | | | | |
| | | | | |
| | | | | |
| | | | | |
| | | | | |
| | | | | |

# ESSENTIAL № 6

# PAPER FILING SYSTEM

Many families keep ten times the amount of paperwork needed. Day after day the mail comes, and day after day the paper clutter grows. In today's digital age there is really no need to hang on to so much paperwork—there are so many ways to maintain and access our needed information digitally, which not only reduces paper waste, but frees us of clutter.

**Things to consider:**

- THE NEW YORK UNIVERSITY SCHOOL OF LAW STATES THAT THE AVERAGE AMERICAN RECEIVES ALMOST 848 PIECES OF JUNK MAIL PER YEAR.

- HARRIS INTERACTIVE REPORTS THAT 23 PERCENT OF ADULTS SAY THEY PAY THEIR BILLS LATE BECAUSE THEY LOSE THEM.

Getting your paper clutter under control and implementing a system will allow you to quickly and efficiently handle new paperwork and digital files, freeing up space in your home and giving you peace of mind.

---

**TIP**

*Be aware that anytime you sign up for offers, subscriptions, raffles, and contests, their goal is often to get you on their mailing list. It is also important to understand that when you fill out warranty cards or register a new product you have purchased, this is also a tactic to get you on their mailing list. To prevent the unwanted and never-ending flow of junk mail when participating in such offers, be sure to incorporate the practice of documenting this statement next to your information: "Please do not trade or sell my name, address, telephone number, and email." If you are on the phone, be sure to verbally state this a few times.*

**STEP ONE:** REDUCE JUNK MAIL

Before we start organizing your paper filing system, it is important to first reduce the amount of unneeded paper that comes into your home. Taking a little time to stop the process of receiving undesired mail and set up systems to minimize the amount of paperwork required for necessary bills and services.

Here are some resources that can help:

| WEBSITE | DESCRIPTION | COMPLETED |
|---|---|---|
| Optoutprescreen.com | A free opt-out service that enables you to stop receiving offers for new credit cards and insurance. | ☐ |
| Catalogchoice.org | An organization on a mission to stop junk mail. They offer a free service to cancel a variety of unwanted paper mail. | ☐ |
| DMAchoice.org | Allows you to screen what unsolicited mail you receive. | ☐ |
| Yellowpagesoptout.com | Opt out of unwanted phone books and catalogs. | ☐ |
| Retailmenot.com/everyday/unsubscribe | Opt out of coupon mailers. | ☐ |
| Valpak.com/coupons/show/mailinglistsuppression | Opt out of Valpak marketing mailers. | ☐ |
| Paperkarma.com | For $1.99 per month this service allows you to snap a photo of your junk mail and submit it, and they will unsubscribe for you. | ☐ |

Now that you have taken the steps to stop junk mail from entering your home, it's important to stay off the "junk mail" list. Follow these steps—the effort is worth it!

| ACTION | MY CREDITORS | COMPLETED |
|---|---|---|
| Contact (call, send an email, or write a letter) all your credit card providers and request that they not share your information, basically requesting to be put on their "in-house" list—a list that is not traded or sold to other companies. | | ☐ ☐ ☐ ☐ ☐ ☐ ☐ |

| ACTION | CHARITY ORGANIZATIONS | COMPLETED |
|---|---|---|
| Contact all the charity organizations that you donate to and request that they only send you one request per year. You might also inquire if they have a paperless option. | | ☐ ☐ ☐ ☐ |

| ACTION | DECEASED | COMPLETED |
|---|---|---|
| Stop mail for deceased family members by writing "Deceased, Return to Sender" on junk mail. Visit DMAchoice.org and register the deceased person on the "Deceased Do Not Contact List." | | ☐ ☐ ☐ ☐ |

| ACTION | PREVIOUS RESIDENT | COMPLETED |
|---|---|---|
| Stop receiving mail for previous residents. Simply writing "Return to Sender" may not resolve the problem. In addition to doing this, also mark through the barcode on the mail, as this is how mail is sorted by the postal service. This will cause the postal service to register the mail as undeliverable. | | ☐ ☐ ☐ ☐ |

# 2 STEP TWO: CHOOSE DIGITAL OR PAPER STATEMENTS

The next step to reducing paper clutter in your home is to decide what system works best for your household to manage statements. There are pros and cons to setting up digital statements versus paper statements. Review the list below to help you decide which is the right choice for your household.

| DIGITAL STATEMENT PROS | DIGITAL STATEMENT CONS |
|---|---|
| Less paper clutter | Must manage account passwords |
| No fees | Easier to miss payments |
| Prevents identify theft | More difficult to catch fraudulent activity |
| Environmentally friendly | Can be blocked by spam filters |
| Accessible from anywhere via the Internet | Changing your address is more time consuming |
| Statements won't get lost in the mail | |

Which did you choose? Use the checklists below to set up a system for managing your digital or paper statements.

| DIGITAL STATEMENTS | ✓ | PAPER STATEMENTS | ✓ |
|---|---|---|---|
| Create a dedicated email for statements and bills | | Set up one location in your home to place all incoming mail (If possible, keep a shredder and recycling bin near this location to quickly discard unnecessary documents.) | |
| Contact all banking institutions and request digital statements | | Assign a family member the responsibility of filing all incoming mail weekly (*Tip: Follow up with this family member each week in your family home meeting to ensure the task is maintained.*) | |
| Contact all credit card companies and request digital statements | | Set a reoccurring date yearly to purge your home files (Use your phone, computer, or planner to remind yourself.) | |
| Create passwords | | Set up a filing system (as explained further in this section) | |
| Keep one paper document on file with account information | | | |
| Ensure that statements are not marked as spam | | | |
| If using auto-pay options, be sure to contact companies to request a specific payment date that coincides with your pay cycle | | | |

### STEP THREE: FILE-SYSTEM PREP

Now that you have set up a system to manage incoming statements and papers, it's time to prep your home paper system setup. First gather all of your paperwork and sort it into stacks following these steps:

- IDENTIFY A SPACE IN YOUR HOME WHERE YOU CAN SORT ALL OF YOUR PAPER-WORK. THIS MAY BE YOUR DINING ROOM TABLE OR A LARGE, OPEN FLOOR SPACE (WHERE FAMILY IS NOT ACTIVELY PASSING THROUGH).

- FOLLOW THE DIAGRAM ON PAGE 115. LAY THEM OUT IN THE SAME FORMAT AS THE DIAGRAM SHOWN.

- ONE FILE AT A TIME, SORT ALL OF YOUR PAPERWORK INTO THE ASSIGNED PILES. COMPLETING THIS TASK AS A FAMILY CAN MAKE THE PROCESS QUICKER. MAKE IT FUN—TURN ON YOUR MUSIC TO BOOST YOUR DRIVE AND MOTIVATION!

Once this task is finished, all your home papers should be in the appropriate pile for its category. It may look overwhelming but know that you are halfway through the process of creating your perfect life-long home filing system.

### STEP FOUR: DECLUTTERING

It is time for the fun to begin! Look at your categorized piles. Using the Decluttering Checklist (pages 116-118), go through each categorized pile. Pull the items on the checklist from the pile; most likely, everything else needs to be placed in the purge, shred, or return pile. If you have items that are not on the checklist, but you feel you should keep, ask yourself this question, and decide based on your answer:

*When is the last time I referenced this? If it has been longer than 2-3 years, get rid of it!*

Use the helpful worksheets and templates at the end of this section to record and organize important information you will want to keep with the files in your file cabinet. In addition to the Password Log (pages 120-121) and helpful diagram for organizing your files, you'll find the following worksheets:

- Medical History Form (pages 122-125). Complete a Medical History Form for each member of your family, and place the completed forms in your "Medical" file.

- Medical Contacts Log (page 126). Use this log to keep track of important contact information for medical providers for the members of your family.

- Medication Log (page 127). Use this log to track prescription medications for each member of your family.

- Pet Sitter Notes (pages 128-129). Use this form to provide your pet sitter(s) with all the information they need to care for your pet(s) while you're away from home.

- Pet Medication Tracker (pages 130-131). Use this sheet to keep track of medications your pet takes or requires.

- Pet Grooming Tracker (pages 132-133). Use this worksheet to keep track of when your pet has received grooming services, such as professional bathing, nail trimming, dental cleaning, flea treatment, etc.

- Extended Family Directory (pages 134-135). Use this helpful worksheet to keep track of contact information for your extended family members.

- Christmas Card List (pages 136-137). Keep track of the names and addresses of the families to whom you send Christmas cards each year.

## STEP SIX: ORGANIZE YOUR SYSTEM

Now that all your items are decluttered and categorized, it is time to choose a storage option that accommodates your home filing needs.

The first important step is to get a fire-proof box for your vital records. The original vital record documents should be kept in this fire-proof box and copies on file. Copies are great to keep in the event that family members need them (registering for school, applying for a job etc.). The size of your household will determine the size of the firebox needed. Many boxes come with the option to use hanging files, which makes it easy to keep original documents tidy.

> **TIP**
>
> *When traveling internationally, always take a copy of your passport along with your original. Do not pack them in the same location. In the event that you lose your passport (or it gets stolen), this will make it easier to get a replacement.*

There are a few different options for storing your home files. The most common is the traditonal file cabinet with hanging files. Another filing option is to use binders. With this system, you will label each folder to correspond with one of the categories on page 115.

Whatever system you choose, it is important to label each file or binder according to its category.

Once you have your system in place, simply file each category in its appropriately labeled binder or file. So easy!

### STEP SEVEN: MAINTAIN YOUR SYSTEM

Now that your home filing system is beautifully organized, you want to keep it that way. Set aside one day a year to go through your file cabinet and purge any old items and add/account for any missing items, such as adding birth certificates and SSN cards for new family members, ensuring that all insurance policies are updated and on file, etc. Continue to use the checklist in this planner as your guide.

# FILE SYSTEM PREP

## — CHECKLIST —

| AUTOMOBILE | BANKING | CHARITY | CHURCH | CREDIT CARDS |
|---|---|---|---|---|
|  |  |  |  |  |

| HOME MAINT. | INSURANCE | INVESTMENTS | LOANS | MEDICAL |
|---|---|---|---|---|
|  |  |  |  |  |

| PET RECORDS | REAL ESTATE | RECEIPTS | SCHOOL | TAXES |
|---|---|---|---|---|
|  |  |    | |  |

| USER MANUALS | UTILITIES | VITAL RECORDS | WARRANTIES | WILLS |
|---|---|---|---|---|
|  |  |  |  |  |

| WORK | MISC. | RECYCLE | PURGE | SHRED |
|---|---|---|---|---|
|  |  |  |  |  |

# DECLUTTERING

If any of the items are missing from your stack, place a sticky note on top of the pile with the name of the missing paper so that you can get it added to the file.

| AUTOMOBILE / TRANSPORTATION | BANKING |
|---|---|
| • Titles<br>• Auto loan agreements<br>• Spare keys<br>• Frequent flyer club<br>• Recreation vehicle information<br>*Note: Auto maintenance records are often kept by your service provider, and your copy can be kept in the glove compartment of your automobile* | • Bank account numbers<br>• Most current bank statement (There is no need to keep multiple bank statements, as most banks offer them online.)<br>• Checkbooks<br>• Deposit slips<br>• Lease and key for safety deposit box |
| **CHARITY** | **CHURCH** |
| • Current church tithing statement<br>• Donation receipts for the current year | • Baptism records<br>• Confirmation records<br>• Church membership documents |
| **CREDIT** | **HOME MAINTENANCE** |
| • Most current statement for each card<br>• Credit contracts<br>• Most recent credit report | • Receipts for all services completed on your home |
| **INSURANCE POLICIES** | **INVESTMENTS** |
| • Homeowner/rental policies<br>• Life policies (all family members)<br>• Automobile policies<br>• Spending plans<br>• Health insurance policies<br>• Disability insurance<br>• Personal liability insurance<br>• Travel insurance policies<br>• Pet insurance | • Retirement/401k statements<br>• Pension plans<br>• Savings bonds<br>• IRA statements |

| LEGAL | LOANS |
|---|---|
| • Divorce decrees<br>• Power of Attorney | • Loan contracts<br>• Student loan contracts<br>• Most current statement for each loan |

| MEDICAL | BILLS |
|---|---|
| • Most recent copy of all family member medical records<br>  (*NOTE: You can often request electronic copies of your medical records from your health provider.*)<br>• Immunization records<br>• Medical history form (pages 122-125)<br>• Medical contacts log (page 126)<br>• Medication log (page 127) | • Home budget spreadsheet<br>• Incoming bills (shred after bill is paid)<br>• Memberships and subscriptions |

| EMERGENCY | PET RECORDS |
|---|---|
| • Family Member Contacts (page 29)<br>• Emergency Contacts (pages 30-32)<br>• Emergency Action Plan (page 33)<br>• Insurance Providers (pages 36-37)<br>• Home Inventory Log (pages 38-39)<br>• Family Member Profile (pages 40-43)<br>• Pet Profiles (pages 44-45) | • Proof of ownership<br>• Spare identification tags<br>• Veterinary health records<br>• Vaccine records<br>• Legal trust<br>• Emergency numbers |

| REAL ESTATE | RECEIPTS |
|---|---|
| • Rental agreements<br>• Property deeds<br>• Home purchase documents<br>• Copy of home title (keep original in safety deposit box)<br>• Tenant agreements (for rental properties)<br>• Spare home keys | • Current receipts within their return window<br>• If keeping receipts for tax purposes, scan or file by month in the tax binder |

| SCHOOL | TAXES |
|---|---|
| • Degrees (originals or copies)<br>• School transcripts<br>• IEP records | • Receipts<br>• Current year tax documents<br>• Previous tax returns (consult tax advisor on how many years to keep) |

| USER MANUALS | UTILITIES |
|---|---|
| • User manuals for items for which the manual is not available online and new items that are still within their return window | • Utility service account numbers |

| VITAL RECORDS | WARRANTIES |
|---|---|
| • Family birth certificates (copy)<br>• Adoption papers (copy)<br>• Healthcare proxy<br>• Citizenship and naturalization paperwork (copy)<br>• Marriage licenses (copy)<br>• Death certificates (copy)<br>• Social security cards (copy)<br>• Driver's licenses (copy)<br>• Passport (copy)<br>*NOTE: Originals for the above should be kept in a fireproof box.* | • Warranties that have not expired |

| WILLS & TRUST | WORK |
|---|---|
| • Wills for household<br>• Trust<br>• Funeral statements/plans, burial records, and plans<br>• Family member contact information (page 29) | • Employment records/appraisals<br>• Employment separation records<br>• Military discharge papers<br>• Service and veteran benefits |

| OTHER | OTHER |
|---|---|
| | |

| OTHER | OTHER |
|---|---|
| | |

# PASSWORD LOG

| COMPANY: | COMPANY: |
|---|---|
| WEBSITE: | WEBSITE: |
| USERNAME: | USERNAME: |
| PASSWORD: | PASSWORD: |
| LINKED EMAIL: | LINKED EMAIL: |
| MEMBERSHIP EXPIRATION DATE: | MEMBERSHIP EXPIRATION DATE: |
| COMPANY: | COMPANY: |
| WEBSITE: | WEBSITE: |
| USERNAME: | USERNAME: |
| PASSWORD: | PASSWORD: |
| LINKED EMAIL: | LINKED EMAIL: |
| MEMBERSHIP EXPIRATION DATE: | MEMBERSHIP EXPIRATION DATE: |
| COMPANY: | COMPANY: |
| WEBSITE: | WEBSITE: |
| USERNAME: | USERNAME: |
| PASSWORD: | PASSWORD: |
| LINKED EMAIL: | LINKED EMAIL: |
| MEMBERSHIP EXPIRATION DATE: | MEMBERSHIP EXPIRATION DATE: |
| COMPANY: | COMPANY: |
| WEBSITE: | WEBSITE: |
| USERNAME: | USERNAME: |
| PASSWORD: | PASSWORD: |
| LINKED EMAIL: | LINKED EMAIL: |
| LINKED EMAIL: | LINKED EMAIL: |
| MEMBERSHIP EXPIRATION DATE: | MEMBERSHIP EXPIRATION DATE: |

# PASSWORD LOG

| COMPANY: | COMPANY: |
|---|---|
| WEBSITE: | WEBSITE: |
| USERNAME: | USERNAME: |
| PASSWORD: | PASSWORD: |
| LINKED EMAIL: | LINKED EMAIL: |
| MEMBERSHIP EXPIRATION DATE: | MEMBERSHIP EXPIRATION DATE: |
| COMPANY: | COMPANY: |
| WEBSITE: | WEBSITE: |
| USERNAME: | USERNAME: |
| PASSWORD: | PASSWORD: |
| LINKED EMAIL: | LINKED EMAIL: |
| MEMBERSHIP EXPIRATION DATE: | MEMBERSHIP EXPIRATION DATE: |
| COMPANY: | COMPANY: |
| WEBSITE: | WEBSITE: |
| USERNAME: | USERNAME: |
| PASSWORD: | PASSWORD: |
| LINKED EMAIL: | LINKED EMAIL: |
| MEMBERSHIP EXPIRATION DATE: | MEMBERSHIP EXPIRATION DATE: |
| COMPANY: | COMPANY: |
| WEBSITE: | WEBSITE: |
| USERNAME: | USERNAME: |
| PASSWORD: | PASSWORD: |
| LINKED EMAIL: | LINKED EMAIL: |
| LINKED EMAIL: | LINKED EMAIL: |
| MEMBERSHIP EXPIRATION DATE: | MEMBERSHIP EXPIRATION DATE: |

# PASSWORD LOG

| COMPANY: | | COMPANY: | |
|---|---|---|---|
| WEBSITE: | | WEBSITE: | |
| USERNAME: | | USERNAME: | |
| PASSWORD: | | PASSWORD: | |
| LINKED EMAIL: | | LINKED EMAIL: | |
| MEMBERSHIP EXPIRATION DATE: | | MEMBERSHIP EXPIRATION DATE: | |
| COMPANY: | | COMPANY: | |
| WEBSITE: | | WEBSITE: | |
| USERNAME: | | USERNAME: | |
| PASSWORD: | | PASSWORD: | |
| LINKED EMAIL: | | LINKED EMAIL: | |
| MEMBERSHIP EXPIRATION DATE: | | MEMBERSHIP EXPIRATION DATE: | |
| COMPANY: | | COMPANY: | |
| WEBSITE: | | WEBSITE: | |
| USERNAME: | | USERNAME: | |
| PASSWORD: | | PASSWORD: | |
| LINKED EMAIL: | | LINKED EMAIL: | |
| MEMBERSHIP EXPIRATION DATE: | | MEMBERSHIP EXPIRATION DATE: | |
| COMPANY: | | COMPANY: | |
| WEBSITE: | | WEBSITE: | |
| USERNAME: | | USERNAME: | |
| PASSWORD: | | PASSWORD: | |
| LINKED EMAIL: | | LINKED EMAIL: | |
| LINKED EMAIL: | | LINKED EMAIL: | |
| MEMBERSHIP EXPIRATION DATE: | | MEMBERSHIP EXPIRATION DATE: | |

# MEDICAL HISTORY FORM

| NAME | DATE OF BIRTH |
|---|---|
| **BLOOD TYPE**<br>☐ O+  ☐ O-  ☐ A+  ☐ A-  ☐ B+  ☐ B-  ☐ AB+  ☐ AB- | **ALLERGIES** |

| MOTHER'S HEALTH HISTORY | | | |
|---|---|---|---|
| RELATIVE | NAME | ILLNESS | NOTES |
| MOTHER | | | |
| GRANDMOTHER | | | |
| GRANDFATHER | | | |

| FATHER'S HEALTH HISTORY | | | |
|---|---|---|---|
| RELATIVE | NAME | ILLNESS | NOTES |
| MOTHER | | | |
| GRANDMOTHER | | | |
| GRANDFATHER | | | |

| IMMEDIATE FAMILY HEALTH HISTORY | | | |
|---|---|---|---|
| RELATIVE | NAME | ILLNESS | NOTES |
| | | | |
| | | | |
| | | | |

# MEDICAL HISTORY FORM

| NAME | DATE OF BIRTH |
|---|---|
| **BLOOD TYPE**<br>☐ O+  ☐ O-  ☐ A+  ☐ A-  ☐ B+  ☐ B-  ☐ AB+  ☐ AB- | **ALLERGIES** |

| MOTHER'S HEALTH HISTORY | | | |
|---|---|---|---|
| RELATIVE | NAME | ILLNESS | NOTES |
| MOTHER | | | |
| GRANDMOTHER | | | |
| GRANDFATHER | | | |

| FATHER'S HEALTH HISTORY | | | |
|---|---|---|---|
| RELATIVE | NAME | ILLNESS | NOTES |
| MOTHER | | | |
| GRANDMOTHER | | | |
| GRANDFATHER | | | |

| IMMEDIATE FAMILY HEALTH HISTORY | | | |
|---|---|---|---|
| RELATIVE | NAME | ILLNESS | NOTES |
| | | | |
| | | | |
| | | | |

# MEDICAL HISTORY FORM

| NAME | DATE OF BIRTH |
|---|---|
| **BLOOD TYPE**<br>□ O+   □ O-   □ A+   □ A-   □ B+   □ B-   □ AB+   □ AB- | **ALLERGIES** |

| MOTHER'S HEALTH HISTORY | | | |
|---|---|---|---|
| **RELATIVE** | **NAME** | **ILLNESS** | **NOTES** |
| MOTHER | | | |
| GRANDMOTHER | | | |
| GRANDFATHER | | | |

| FATHER'S HEALTH HISTORY | | | |
|---|---|---|---|
| **RELATIVE** | **NAME** | **ILLNESS** | **NOTES** |
| MOTHER | | | |
| GRANDMOTHER | | | |
| GRANDFATHER | | | |

| IMMEDIATE FAMILY HEALTH HISTORY | | | |
|---|---|---|---|
| **RELATIVE** | **NAME** | **ILLNESS** | **NOTES** |
| | | | |
| | | | |
| | | | |

# MEDICAL HISTORY FORM

| NAME | DATE OF BIRTH |
|------|---------------|
| **BLOOD TYPE**<br>☐ O+   ☐ O-   ☐ A+   ☐ A-   ☐ B+   ☐ B-   ☐ AB+   ☐ AB- | **ALLERGIES** |

| MOTHER'S HEALTH HISTORY | | | |
|------------------------|---|---|---|
| RELATIVE | NAME | ILLNESS | NOTES |
| MOTHER | | | |
| GRANDMOTHER | | | |
| GRANDFATHER | | | |

| FATHER'S HEALTH HISTORY | | | |
|------------------------|---|---|---|
| RELATIVE | NAME | ILLNESS | NOTES |
| MOTHER | | | |
| GRANDMOTHER | | | |
| GRANDFATHER | | | |

| IMMEDIATE FAMILY HEALTH HISTORY | | | |
|--------------------------------|---|---|---|
| RELATIVE | NAME | ILLNESS | NOTES |
| | | | |
| | | | |
| | | | |

# MEDICAL CONTACTS LOG

| FAMILY MEMBER | MEDICAL PROVIDER NAME | SPECIALTY | PHONE NUMBER | ADDRESS |
|---|---|---|---|---|
| | | | | |
| | | | | |
| | | | | |
| | | | | |
| | | | | |
| | | | | |
| | | | | |
| | | | | |
| | | | | |
| | | | | |
| | | | | |
| | | | | |
| | | | | |
| | | | | |
| | | | | |
| | | | | |
| | | | | |
| | | | | |
| | | | | |

# MEDICATION LOG

| NAME: | | | | | | |
|-------|--------|------|-----------|--------------------|----------------------|-----------------------|
| MEDICATION | DOSAGE | TIME | PHYSICIAN | MEDICATION PURPOSE | POSSIBLE SIDE EFFECTS | PRESCRIPTION END DATE |
| | | | | | | |
| | | | | | | |
| | | | | | | |
| | | | | | | |
| | | | | | | |
| | | | | | | |
| | | | | | | |
| | | | | | | |
| | | | | | | |
| | | | | | | |
| | | | | | | |
| | | | | | | |
| | | | | | | |
| | | | | | | |
| | | | | | | |
| | | | | | | |
| | | | | | | |
| | | | | | | |
| | | | | | | |

CLOSE-UP

IMAGE

OF

PET

HERE

| NAME: | | |
|---|---|---|
| AGE: | | |
| GENDER: | | |
| BREED / COLOR: | | |
| MICROCHIP ID: | | |
| MICROCHIP REGISTERED WITH: | | |
| ALLERGIES: | | |
| MEDICATIONS: | | |
| FOOD AMOUNT: | FEEDING TIMES: | |
| BRAND OF FOOD: | | |
| WATER: ☐ UNLIMITED | | |
| TREATS: | | |
| TABLE FOOD ALLOWED: ☐ YES ☐ NO | | |
| MEDICAL ISSUES: | | |

**MORNING ROUTINE**

**AFTERNOON ROUTINE**

**NIGHT ROUTINE**

**VETERINARIAN**

| NAME | PHONE | ADDRESS |
|---|---|---|
| | | |

**EMERGENCY CONTACTS**

| NAME | PHONE | ADDRESS |
|---|---|---|
| | | |
| | | |

# PET SITTER NOTES

CLOSE-UP

IMAGE

OF

PET

HERE

| | |
|---|---|
| **NAME:** | |
| **AGE:** | |
| **GENDER:** | |
| **BREED / COLOR:** | |
| **MICROCHIP ID:** | |
| **MICROCHIP REGISTERED WITH:** | |
| **ALLERGIES:** | |
| **MEDICATIONS:** | |
| **FOOD AMOUNT:** | **FEEDING TIMES:** |
| **BRAND OF FOOD:** | |
| **WATER:** ☐ UNLIMITED | |
| **TREATS:** | |
| **TABLE FOOD ALLOWED:** ☐ YES ☐ NO | |
| **MEDICAL ISSUES:** | |

**MORNING ROUTINE**

**AFTERNOON ROUTINE**

**NIGHT ROUTINE**

**VETERINARIAN**

| NAME | PHONE | ADDRESS |
|---|---|---|
| | | |

**EMERGENCY CONTACTS**

| NAME | PHONE | ADDRESS |
|---|---|---|
| | | |
| | | |

# PET MEDICATION TRACKER

| PET NAME | BIRTHDAY | BREED / COLOR |
|---|---|---|
|  |  |  |

| MEDICATIONS | | | | | |
|---|---|---|---|---|---|
| DATE | TIME | MEDICATION | DOSAGE | FREQUENCY | VET |
|  |  |  |  |  |  |
|  |  |  |  |  |  |
|  |  |  |  |  |  |
|  |  |  |  |  |  |
|  |  |  |  |  |  |
|  |  |  |  |  |  |
|  |  |  |  |  |  |
|  |  |  |  |  |  |
|  |  |  |  |  |  |
|  |  |  |  |  |  |
|  |  |  |  |  |  |
|  |  |  |  |  |  |
|  |  |  |  |  |  |
|  |  |  |  |  |  |
|  |  |  |  |  |  |
|  |  |  |  |  |  |
|  |  |  |  |  |  |
|  |  |  |  |  |  |
|  |  |  |  |  |  |
|  |  |  |  |  |  |
|  |  |  |  |  |  |
|  |  |  |  |  |  |
|  |  |  |  |  |  |

# PET MEDICATION TRACKER

| PET NAME | BIRTHDAY | BREED / COLOR |
|----------|----------|---------------|
|          |          |               |

| MEDICATIONS | | | | | |
|------|------|------------|--------|-----------|-----|
| DATE | TIME | MEDICATION | DOSAGE | FREQUENCY | VET |
|      |      |            |        |           |     |
|      |      |            |        |           |     |
|      |      |            |        |           |     |
|      |      |            |        |           |     |
|      |      |            |        |           |     |
|      |      |            |        |           |     |
|      |      |            |        |           |     |
|      |      |            |        |           |     |
|      |      |            |        |           |     |
|      |      |            |        |           |     |
|      |      |            |        |           |     |
|      |      |            |        |           |     |
|      |      |            |        |           |     |
|      |      |            |        |           |     |
|      |      |            |        |           |     |
|      |      |            |        |           |     |
|      |      |            |        |           |     |
|      |      |            |        |           |     |
|      |      |            |        |           |     |
|      |      |            |        |           |     |
|      |      |            |        |           |     |
|      |      |            |        |           |     |

# PET GROOMING TRACKER

| PET NAME | BIRTHDAY | BREED / COLOR |
|----------|----------|---------------|
|          |          |               |

| DATE | TIME | SERVICE | LOCATION | COST |
|------|------|---------|----------|------|
|  |  | ☐ BATH   ☐ EAR CLEANING   ☐ NAILS   ☐ BRUSH<br>☐ HAIRCUT   ☐ DEMATTING   ☐ TEETH BRUSHING<br>☐ FLEA TREATMENT   ☐ OTHER |  |  |
|  |  | ☐ BATH   ☐ EAR CLEANING   ☐ NAILS   ☐ BRUSH<br>☐ HAIRCUT   ☐ DEMATTING   ☐ TEETH BRUSHING<br>☐ FLEA TREATMENT   ☐ OTHER |  |  |
|  |  | ☐ BATH   ☐ EAR CLEANING   ☐ NAILS   ☐ BRUSH<br>☐ HAIRCUT   ☐ DEMATTING   ☐ TEETH BRUSHING<br>☐ FLEA TREATMENT   ☐ OTHER |  |  |
|  |  | ☐ BATH   ☐ EAR CLEANING   ☐ NAILS   ☐ BRUSH<br>☐ HAIRCUT   ☐ DEMATTING   ☐ TEETH BRUSHING<br>☐ FLEA TREATMENT   ☐ OTHER |  |  |
|  |  | ☐ BATH   ☐ EAR CLEANING   ☐ NAILS   ☐ BRUSH<br>☐ HAIRCUT   ☐ DEMATTING   ☐ TEETH BRUSHING<br>☐ FLEA TREATMENT   ☐ OTHER |  |  |
|  |  | ☐ BATH   ☐ EAR CLEANING   ☐ NAILS   ☐ BRUSH<br>☐ HAIRCUT   ☐ DEMATTING   ☐ TEETH BRUSHING<br>☐ FLEA TREATMENT   ☐ OTHER |  |  |
|  |  | ☐ BATH   ☐ EAR CLEANING   ☐ NAILS   ☐ BRUSH<br>☐ HAIRCUT   ☐ DEMATTING   ☐ TEETH BRUSHING<br>☐ FLEA TREATMENT   ☐ OTHER |  |  |
|  |  | ☐ BATH   ☐ EAR CLEANING   ☐ NAILS   ☐ BRUSH<br>☐ HAIRCUT   ☐ DEMATTING   ☐ TEETH BRUSHING<br>☐ FLEA TREATMENT   ☐ OTHER |  |  |
|  |  | ☐ BATH   ☐ EAR CLEANING   ☐ NAILS   ☐ BRUSH<br>☐ HAIRCUT   ☐ DEMATTING   ☐ TEETH BRUSHING<br>☐ FLEA TREATMENT   ☐ OTHER |  |  |
|  |  | ☐ BATH   ☐ EAR CLEANING   ☐ NAILS   ☐ BRUSH<br>☐ HAIRCUT   ☐ DEMATTING   ☐ TEETH BRUSHING<br>☐ FLEA TREATMENT   ☐ OTHER |  |  |
|  |  | ☐ BATH   ☐ EAR CLEANING   ☐ NAILS   ☐ BRUSH<br>☐ HAIRCUT   ☐ DEMATTING   ☐ TEETH BRUSHING<br>☐ FLEA TREATMENT   ☐ OTHER |  |  |

# PET GROOMING TRACKER

| PET NAME | BIRTHDAY | BREED / COLOR |
|---|---|---|
|  |  |  |

| DATE | TIME | SERVICE | LOCATION | COST |
|---|---|---|---|---|
|  |  | ☐ BATH  ☐ EAR CLEANING  ☐ NAILS  ☐ BRUSH  ☐ HAIRCUT  ☐ DEMATTING  ☐ TEETH BRUSHING  ☐ FLEA TREATMENT  ☐ OTHER |  |  |
|  |  | ☐ BATH  ☐ EAR CLEANING  ☐ NAILS  ☐ BRUSH  ☐ HAIRCUT  ☐ DEMATTING  ☐ TEETH BRUSHING  ☐ FLEA TREATMENT  ☐ OTHER |  |  |
|  |  | ☐ BATH  ☐ EAR CLEANING  ☐ NAILS  ☐ BRUSH  ☐ HAIRCUT  ☐ DEMATTING  ☐ TEETH BRUSHING  ☐ FLEA TREATMENT  ☐ OTHER |  |  |
|  |  | ☐ BATH  ☐ EAR CLEANING  ☐ NAILS  ☐ BRUSH  ☐ HAIRCUT  ☐ DEMATTING  ☐ TEETH BRUSHING  ☐ FLEA TREATMENT  ☐ OTHER |  |  |
|  |  | ☐ BATH  ☐ EAR CLEANING  ☐ NAILS  ☐ BRUSH  ☐ HAIRCUT  ☐ DEMATTING  ☐ TEETH BRUSHING  ☐ FLEA TREATMENT  ☐ OTHER |  |  |
|  |  | ☐ BATH  ☐ EAR CLEANING  ☐ NAILS  ☐ BRUSH  ☐ HAIRCUT  ☐ DEMATTING  ☐ TEETH BRUSHING  ☐ FLEA TREATMENT  ☐ OTHER |  |  |
|  |  | ☐ BATH  ☐ EAR CLEANING  ☐ NAILS  ☐ BRUSH  ☐ HAIRCUT  ☐ DEMATTING  ☐ TEETH BRUSHING  ☐ FLEA TREATMENT  ☐ OTHER |  |  |
|  |  | ☐ BATH  ☐ EAR CLEANING  ☐ NAILS  ☐ BRUSH  ☐ HAIRCUT  ☐ DEMATTING  ☐ TEETH BRUSHING  ☐ FLEA TREATMENT  ☐ OTHER |  |  |
|  |  | ☐ BATH  ☐ EAR CLEANING  ☐ NAILS  ☐ BRUSH  ☐ HAIRCUT  ☐ DEMATTING  ☐ TEETH BRUSHING  ☐ FLEA TREATMENT  ☐ OTHER |  |  |
|  |  | ☐ BATH  ☐ EAR CLEANING  ☐ NAILS  ☐ BRUSH  ☐ HAIRCUT  ☐ DEMATTING  ☐ TEETH BRUSHING  ☐ FLEA TREATMENT  ☐ OTHER |  |  |
|  |  | ☐ BATH  ☐ EAR CLEANING  ☐ NAILS  ☐ BRUSH  ☐ HAIRCUT  ☐ DEMATTING  ☐ TEETH BRUSHING  ☐ FLEA TREATMENT  ☐ OTHER |  |  |

# EXTENDED FAMILY DIRECTORY

| NAME: | NAME: |
|---|---|
| RELATION: | RELATION: |
| ADDRESS: | ADDRESS: |
| HOME PHONE: | HOME PHONE: |
| MOBILE PHONE: | MOBILE PHONE: |
| EMAIL: | EMAIL: |
| SPOUSE'S NAME: | SPOUSE'S NAME: |
| SPOUSE'S MOBILE PHONE: | SPOUSE'S MOBILE PHONE: |
| BIRTHDAY: | BIRTHDAY: |
| ANNIVERSARY: | ANNIVERSARY: |

| NAME: | NAME: |
|---|---|
| RELATION: | RELATION: |
| ADDRESS: | ADDRESS: |
| HOME PHONE: | HOME PHONE: |
| MOBILE PHONE: | MOBILE PHONE: |
| EMAIL: | EMAIL: |
| SPOUSE'S NAME: | SPOUSE'S NAME: |
| SPOUSE'S MOBILE PHONE: | SPOUSE'S MOBILE PHONE: |
| BIRTHDAY: | BIRTHDAY: |
| ANNIVERSARY: | ANNIVERSARY: |

| NAME: | NAME: |
|---|---|
| RELATION: | RELATION: |
| ADDRESS: | ADDRESS: |
| HOME PHONE: | HOME PHONE: |
| MOBILE PHONE: | MOBILE PHONE: |
| EMAIL: | EMAIL: |
| SPOUSE'S NAME: | SPOUSE'S NAME: |
| SPOUSE'S MOBILE PHONE: | SPOUSE'S MOBILE PHONE: |
| BIRTHDAY: | BIRTHDAY: |
| ANNIVERSARY: | ANNIVERSARY: |

# EXTENDED FAMILY DIRECTORY

| | | |
|---|---|---|
| NAME: | | NAME: |
| RELATION: | | RELATION: |
| ADDRESS: | | ADDRESS: |
| HOME PHONE: | | HOME PHONE: |
| MOBILE PHONE: | | MOBILE PHONE: |
| EMAIL: | | EMAIL: |
| SPOUSE'S NAME: | | SPOUSE'S NAME: |
| SPOUSE'S MOBILE PHONE: | | SPOUSE'S MOBILE PHONE: |
| BIRTHDAY: | | BIRTHDAY: |
| ANNIVERSARY: | | ANNIVERSARY: |

| | | |
|---|---|---|
| NAME: | | NAME: |
| RELATION: | | RELATION: |
| ADDRESS: | | ADDRESS: |
| HOME PHONE: | | HOME PHONE: |
| MOBILE PHONE: | | MOBILE PHONE: |
| EMAIL: | | EMAIL: |
| SPOUSE'S NAME: | | SPOUSE'S NAME: |
| SPOUSE'S MOBILE PHONE: | | SPOUSE'S MOBILE PHONE: |
| BIRTHDAY: | | BIRTHDAY: |
| ANNIVERSARY: | | ANNIVERSARY: |

| | | |
|---|---|---|
| NAME: | | NAME: |
| RELATION: | | RELATION: |
| ADDRESS: | | ADDRESS: |
| HOME PHONE: | | HOME PHONE: |
| MOBILE PHONE: | | MOBILE PHONE: |
| EMAIL: | | EMAIL: |
| SPOUSE'S NAME: | | SPOUSE'S NAME: |
| SPOUSE'S MOBILE PHONE: | | SPOUSE'S MOBILE PHONE: |
| BIRTHDAY: | | BIRTHDAY: |
| ANNIVERSARY: | | ANNIVERSARY: |

# CHRISTMAS CARD LIST

| NAME | ADDRESS | SENT |
|------|---------|------|
| | | ☐ |
| | | ☐ |
| | | ☐ |
| | | ☐ |
| | | ☐ |
| | | ☐ |
| | | ☐ |
| | | ☐ |
| | | ☐ |
| | | ☐ |
| | | ☐ |
| | | ☐ |
| | | ☐ |
| | | ☐ |
| | | ☐ |
| | | ☐ |
| | | ☐ |
| | | ☐ |
| | | ☐ |
| | | ☐ |

# CHRISTMAS CARD LIST

| NAME | ADDRESS | SENT |
|------|---------|------|
|  |  | ☐ |
|  |  | ☐ |
|  |  | ☐ |
|  |  | ☐ |
|  |  | ☐ |
|  |  | ☐ |
|  |  | ☐ |
|  |  | ☐ |
|  |  | ☐ |
|  |  | ☐ |
|  |  | ☐ |
|  |  | ☐ |
|  |  | ☐ |
|  |  | ☐ |
|  |  | ☐ |
|  |  | ☐ |
|  |  | ☐ |
|  |  | ☐ |
|  |  | ☐ |
|  |  | ☐ |

# ESSENTIAL №7

## HOME BUDGET

A big part of having a well-organized and well-managed household is having a budget. Financial problems can cause a great deal of stress and upset within a family. A budget is an essential tool to ensure that your family lives within its means and maintains financial security.

A budget also helps you plan for your future, prepare for unexpected emergencies, maximize your savings, and create a better quality of life for you and your children.

Now, let's organize your budget!

# CREATING A HOUSEHOLD BUDGET

## MONTHLY BUDGET

A monthly home budget is a must-have to successfully manage your household finances. A good budget allows you to easily plan for and understand what you owe, what you earn, and what you spend. Budgeting does not have to be a difficult or grueling experience each month!

Now, let's set up a simplified monthly budget for your household. Use the Monthly Budget Worksheet (pages 142-143) to organize your monthly income, expenses, and savings.

## YEARLY BUDGET

Keeping a yearly overview of your budget is a great way to capture your entire financial year in one glance. This is great for identifying months in which your expenses are higher, which allows you to better structure your budget and savings. It's also a motivator for how much you save over the months and acts as a tool you can use to challenge yourself to make the next month's budget better than the previous months. Use the yearly Yearly Budget Worksheet (page 144) to capture your yearly budget.

## EMERGENCY FUND

Unexpected expenses are an easy way to destroy your household budget and go into debt. Having an emergency fund in place for unexpected expenses will provide your household with the financial security it needs to run smoothly. It is generally recommended that you build your emergency fund to cover three to six months of expenses. Use the Emergency Fund tracker (page 145) to track your emergency fund.

## SINKING FUNDS

Sinking funds are a preventive measure that keeps you from destroying your budget. The idea is to set up a mini savings account for all your expected extra expenses, such as holidays, birthdays, back-to-school, annual vehicle registration, repair expenses, etc.

Use the Sinking Fund Tracker Worksheets (pages 146-150) to track the funds you set aside for expenses in these categories.

## SAVINGS CHALLENGE

Saving challenges are a wonderful way to get the funds into your savings accounts without overwhelming your pocket in a way that does not feel overwhelming.

Saving challenges are structured to help you to save in small increments over a short period of time (usually a year). They also make you think twice about small unnecessary expenses like grabbing that six-dollar latte five days a week.

The Savings Challenges (pages 151-153) cover a variety of saving goals. Find one or two that fit you best, and let the savings begin!

## SUBSCRIPTION TRACKING

Many of us love our subscriptions, from newspapers and magazines to subscription box services. Grouping all your subscriptions together helps you easily identify potential services you no longer desire and allows you to gain a better perspective on the amount of money you spend on subscriptions as a whole.

Use the handy Subscription Tracker (page 154) to keep track of all your household subscriptions.

## DEBT PAYMENT TRACKING

Most households need to take on a certain level of debt, but it must be carefully managed. Debt can result in years and years of stress, frustration, and struggle if you do not work diligently to dissolve it. Use the Debt Payment Trackers (pages 155-157) to keep track of all your debt and monitor the process of paying it off.

# MONTHLY BUDGET WORKSHEET

| INCOME | EXPECTED | ACTUAL | DIFFERENCE |
|---|---|---|---|
|  |  |  |  |
|  |  |  |  |
|  |  |  |  |
|  |  |  |  |
| TITHES AND CHARITY | EXPECTED | ACTUAL | DIFFERENCE |
|  |  |  |  |
|  |  |  |  |
|  |  |  |  |
| SAVINGS | EXPECTED | ACTUAL | DIFFERENCE |
|  |  |  |  |
|  |  |  |  |
|  |  |  |  |
|  |  |  |  |
| MORTGAGE / RENT / CAR PAYMENTS | EXPECTED | ACTUAL | DIFFERENCE |
|  |  |  |  |
|  |  |  |  |
|  |  |  |  |
| UTILITIES | EXPECTED | ACTUAL | DIFFERENCE |
|  |  |  |  |
|  |  |  |  |
|  |  |  |  |
|  |  |  |  |
| GROCERIES & HOUSEHOLD ITEMS | EXPECTED | ACTUAL | DIFFERENCE |
|  |  |  |  |
|  |  |  |  |
|  |  |  |  |
|  |  |  |  |
|  |  |  |  |

| GAS/TRANSPORTATION | EXPECTED | ACTUAL | DIFFERENCE |
|---|---|---|---|
| | | | |
| | | | |
| | | | |
| | | | |

| MEDICAL/HEALTH | EXPECTED | ACTUAL | DIFFERENCE |
|---|---|---|---|
| | | | |
| | | | |
| | | | |
| | | | |

| DEBT | EXPECTED | ACTUAL | DIFFERENCE |
|---|---|---|---|
| | | | |
| | | | |
| | | | |

| MEALS OUT / ENTERTAINMENT | EXPECTED | ACTUAL | DIFFERENCE |
|---|---|---|---|
| | | | |
| | | | |
| | | | |

| CLOTHING AND PERSONAL ITEMS | EXPECTED | ACTUAL | DIFFERENCE |
|---|---|---|---|
| | | | |
| | | | |
| | | | |

| SUBSCRIPTIONS | | | |
|---|---|---|---|
| | | | |
| | | | |
| | | | |

| PETS | | | |
|---|---|---|---|
| | | | |
| | | | |
| | | | |

| MONTHLY TOTALS | | | |
|---|---|---|---|
| INCOME | EXPENSES | DIFFERENCE | |
| | | | |

| SAVED |
|---|
| |

## BUDGET WORKSHEET

| JANUARY | FEBRUARY | MARCH |
|---|---|---|
| INCOME: $ | INCOME: $ | INCOME: $ |
| SAVINGS: $ | SAVINGS: $ | SAVINGS: $ |
| DEBT PAYMENTS: $ | DEBT PAYMENTS: $ | DEBT PAYMENTS: $ |
| EXPENSES: $ | EXPENSES: $ | EXPENSES: $ |
| **APRIL** | **MAY** | **JUNE** |
| INCOME: $ | INCOME: $ | INCOME: $ |
| SAVINGS: $ | SAVINGS: $ | SAVINGS: $ |
| DEBT PAYMENTS: $ | DEBT PAYMENTS: $ | DEBT PAYMENTS: $ |
| EXPENSES: $ | EXPENSES: $ | EXPENSES: $ |
| **JULY** | **AUGUST** | **SEPTEMBER** |
| INCOME: $ | INCOME: $ | INCOME: $ |
| SAVINGS: $ | SAVINGS: $ | SAVINGS: $ |
| DEBT PAYMENTS: $ | DEBT PAYMENTS: $ | DEBT PAYMENTS: $ |
| EXPENSES: $ | EXPENSES: $ | EXPENSES: $ |
| **OCTOBER** | **NOVEMBER** | **DECEMBER** |
| INCOME: $ | INCOME: $ | INCOME: $ |
| SAVINGS: $ | SAVINGS: $ | SAVINGS: $ |
| DEBT PAYMENTS: $ | DEBT PAYMENTS: $ | DEBT PAYMENTS: $ |
| EXPENSES: $ | EXPENSES: $ | EXPENSES: $ |

# EMERGENCY

## FUND TRACKER

| MONTH | DEPOSIT | WITHDRAWAL | WITHDRAWAL REASON | BALANCE |
|---|---|---|---|---|
| JANUARY | | | | |
| FEBRUARY | | | | |
| MARCH | | | | |
| APRIL | | | | |
| MAY | | | | |
| JUNE | | | | |
| JULY | | | | |
| AUGUST | | | | |
| SEPTEMBER | | | | |
| OCTOBER | | | | |
| NOVEMBER | | | | |
| DECEMBER | | | | |
| **ACCOUNT INFORMATION** | | | | |
| BANK NAME: | | | | |
| ACCOUNT TYPE: | | | | |
| ACCOUNT WEBSITE: | | | | |
| BANK WEBSITE: | | | | |
| BANK TELEPHONE: | | | | |
| USERNAME: | | | | |
| PASSWORD: | | | | |

# HOLIDAY SINKING FUND TRACKER

| MONTH | DEPOSIT AMOUNT | WITHDRAWAL AMOUNT | BALANCE |
|---|---|---|---|
| JANUARY | | | |
| FEBRUARY | | | |
| MARCH | | | |
| APRIL | | | |
| MAY | | | |
| JUNE | | | |
| JULY | | | |
| AUGUST | | | |
| SEPTEMBER | | | |
| OCTOBER | | | |
| NOVEMBER | | | |
| DECEMBER | | | |

# VACATION SINKING FUND TRACKER

| MONTH | DEPOSIT AMOUNT | WITHDRAWAL AMOUNT | BALANCE |
|---|---|---|---|
| JANUARY | | | |
| FEBRUARY | | | |
| MARCH | | | |
| APRIL | | | |
| MAY | | | |
| JUNE | | | |
| JULY | | | |
| AUGUST | | | |
| SEPTEMBER | | | |
| OCTOBER | | | |
| NOVEMBER | | | |
| DECEMBER | | | |

# GIFTS SINKING FUND TRACKER

| MONTH | DEPOSIT AMOUNT | WITHDRAWAL AMOUNT | BALANCE |
|---|---|---|---|
| JANUARY | | | |
| FEBRUARY | | | |
| MARCH | | | |
| APRIL | | | |
| MAY | | | |
| JUNE | | | |
| JULY | | | |
| AUGUST | | | |
| SEPTEMBER | | | |
| OCTOBER | | | |
| NOVEMBER | | | |
| DECEMBER | | | |

# BACK-TO-SCHOOL SINKING FUND TRACKER

| MONTH | DEPOSIT AMOUNT | WITHDRAWAL AMOUNT | BALANCE |
|---|---|---|---|
| JANUARY | | | |
| FEBRUARY | | | |
| MARCH | | | |
| APRIL | | | |
| MAY | | | |
| JUNE | | | |
| JULY | | | |
| AUGUST | | | |
| SEPTEMBER | | | |
| OCTOBER | | | |
| NOVEMBER | | | |
| DECEMBER | | | |

## VEHICLES SINKING FUND TRACKER

| MONTH | DEPOSIT AMOUNT | WITHDRAWAL AMOUNT | BALANCE |
|---|---|---|---|
| JANUARY | | | |
| FEBRUARY | | | |
| MARCH | | | |
| APRIL | | | |
| MAY | | | |
| JUNE | | | |
| JULY | | | |
| AUGUST | | | |
| SEPTEMBER | | | |
| OCTOBER | | | |
| NOVEMBER | | | |
| DECEMBER | | | |

## MEDICAL / DENTAL SINKING FUND TRACKER

| MONTH | DEPOSIT AMOUNT | WITHDRAWAL AMOUNT | BALANCE |
|---|---|---|---|
| JANUARY | | | |
| FEBRUARY | | | |
| MARCH | | | |
| APRIL | | | |
| MAY | | | |
| JUNE | | | |
| JULY | | | |
| AUGUST | | | |
| SEPTEMBER | | | |
| OCTOBER | | | |
| NOVEMBER | | | |
| DECEMBER | | | |

## PETS SINKING FUND TRACKER

| MONTH | DEPOSIT AMOUNT | WITHDRAWAL AMOUNT | BALANCE |
|---|---|---|---|
| JANUARY | | | |
| FEBRUARY | | | |
| MARCH | | | |
| APRIL | | | |
| MAY | | | |
| JUNE | | | |
| JULY | | | |
| AUGUST | | | |
| SEPTEMBER | | | |
| OCTOBER | | | |
| NOVEMBER | | | |
| DECEMBER | | | |

## _____ SINKING FUND TRACKER

| MONTH | DEPOSIT AMOUNT | WITHDRAWAL AMOUNT | BALANCE |
|---|---|---|---|
| JANUARY | | | |
| FEBRUARY | | | |
| MARCH | | | |
| APRIL | | | |
| MAY | | | |
| JUNE | | | |
| JULY | | | |
| AUGUST | | | |
| SEPTEMBER | | | |
| OCTOBER | | | |
| NOVEMBER | | | |
| DECEMBER | | | |

_____ SINKING FUND TRACKER

| MONTH | DEPOSIT AMOUNT | WITHDRAWAL AMOUNT | BALANCE |
|---|---|---|---|
| JANUARY | | | |
| FEBRUARY | | | |
| MARCH | | | |
| APRIL | | | |
| MAY | | | |
| JUNE | | | |
| JULY | | | |
| AUGUST | | | |
| SEPTEMBER | | | |
| OCTOBER | | | |
| NOVEMBER | | | |
| DECEMBER | | | |

_____ SINKING FUND TRACKER

| MONTH | DEPOSIT AMOUNT | WITHDRAWAL AMOUNT | BALANCE |
|---|---|---|---|
| JANUARY | | | |
| FEBRUARY | | | |
| MARCH | | | |
| APRIL | | | |
| MAY | | | |
| JUNE | | | |
| JULY | | | |
| AUGUST | | | |
| SEPTEMBER | | | |
| OCTOBER | | | |
| NOVEMBER | | | |
| DECEMBER | | | |

# $1,000 YEARLONG SAVINGS CHALLENGE

| WEEK | DEPOSIT | TOTAL | ✓ | WEEK | DEPOSIT | TOTAL | ✓ |
|------|---------|-------|---|------|---------|-------|---|
| 1 | $10.00 | $10.00 | | 27 | $20.00 | $500.00 | |
| 2 | $10.00 | $20.00 | | 28 | $20.00 | $520.00 | |
| 3 | $10.00 | $30.00 | | 29 | $20.00 | $540.00 | |
| 4 | $10.00 | $40.00 | | 30 | $20.00 | $560.00 | |
| 5 | $20.00 | $60.00 | | 31 | $20.00 | $580.00 | |
| 6 | $20.00 | $80.00 | | 32 | $20.00 | $600.00 | |
| 7 | $20.00 | $100.00 | | 33 | $20.00 | $620.00 | |
| 8 | $20.00 | $120.00 | | 34 | $20.00 | $640.00 | |
| 9 | $20.00 | $140.00 | | 35 | $20.00 | $660.00 | |
| 10 | $20.00 | $160.00 | | 36 | $20.00 | $680.00 | |
| 11 | $20.00 | $180.00 | | 37 | $20.00 | $700.00 | |
| 12 | $20.00 | $200.00 | | 38 | $20.00 | $720.00 | |
| 13 | $20.00 | $220.00 | | 39 | $20.00 | $740.00 | |
| 14 | $20.00 | $240.00 | | 40 | $20.00 | $760.00 | |
| 15 | $20.00 | $260.00 | | 41 | $20.00 | $780.00 | |
| 16 | $20.00 | $280.00 | | 42 | $20.00 | $800.00 | |
| 17 | $20.00 | $300.00 | | 43 | $20.00 | $820.00 | |
| 18 | $20.00 | $320.00 | | 44 | $20.00 | $840.00 | |
| 19 | $20.00 | $340.00 | | 45 | $20.00 | $860.00 | |
| 20 | $20.00 | $360.00 | | 46 | $20.00 | $880.00 | |
| 21 | $20.00 | $380.00 | | 47 | $20.00 | $900.00 | |
| 22 | $20.00 | $400.00 | | 48 | $20.00 | $920.00 | |
| 23 | $20.00 | $420.00 | | 49 | $20.00 | $940.00 | |
| 24 | $20.00 | $440.00 | | 50 | $20.00 | $960.00 | |
| 25 | $20.00 | $460.00 | | 51 | $20.00 | $980.00 | |
| 26 | $20.00 | $480.00 | | 52 | $20.00 | $1,000.00 | |

## ACCOUNT INFORMATION

BANK NAME:

ACCOUNT TYPE:

ACCOUNT WEBSITE:          BANK WEBSITE:

BANK TELEPHONE:

USERNAME:          PASSWORD:

# $5,000 YEARLONG SAVINGS CHALLENGE

| WEEK | DEPOSIT | TOTAL | ✓ | WEEK | DEPOSIT | TOTAL | ✓ |
|------|---------|-------|---|------|---------|-------|---|
| 1 | $50.00 | $50.00 | | 27 | $100.00 | $2,900.00 | |
| 2 | $50.00 | $100.00 | | 28 | $100.00 | $3,000.00 | |
| 3 | $50.00 | $150.00 | | 29 | $150.00 | $3,150.00 | |
| 4 | $50.00 | $200.00 | | 30 | $150.00 | $3,300.00 | |
| 5 | $100.00 | $300.00 | | 31 | $150.00 | $3,450.00 | |
| 6 | $100.00 | $400.00 | | 32 | $150.00 | $3,600.00 | |
| 7 | $100.00 | $500.00 | | 33 | $100.00 | $3,700.00 | |
| 8 | $100.00 | $600.00 | | 34 | $100.00 | $3,800.00 | |
| 9 | $200.00 | $800.00 | | 35 | $100.00 | $3,900.00 | |
| 10 | $200.00 | $1,000.00 | | 36 | $100.00 | $4,000.00 | |
| 11 | $200.00 | $1,200.00 | | 37 | $50.00 | $4,050.00 | |
| 12 | $200.00 | $1,400.00 | | 38 | $50.00 | $4,100.00 | |
| 13 | $150.00 | $1,550.00 | | 39 | $50.00 | $4,150.00 | |
| 14 | $150.00 | $1,700.00 | | 40 | $50.00 | $4,200.00 | |
| 15 | $150.00 | $1,850.00 | | 41 | $100.00 | $4,300.00 | |
| 16 | $150.00 | $2,000.00 | | 42 | $100.00 | $4,400.00 | |
| 17 | $100.00 | $2,100.00 | | 43 | $100.00 | $4,500.00 | |
| 18 | $100.00 | $2,200.00 | | 44 | $100.00 | $4,600.00 | |
| 19 | $100.00 | $2,300.00 | | 45 | $50.00 | $4,650.00 | |
| 20 | $100.00 | $2,400.00 | | 46 | $50.00 | $4,700.00 | |
| 21 | $50.00 | $2,450.00 | | 47 | $50.00 | $4,750.00 | |
| 22 | $50.00 | $2,500.00 | | 48 | $50.00 | $4,800.00 | |
| 23 | $50.00 | $2,550.00 | | 49 | $50.00 | $4,850.00 | |
| 24 | $50.00 | $2,600.00 | | 50 | $50.00 | $4,900.00 | |
| 25 | $100.00 | $2,700.00 | | 51 | $50.00 | $4,950.00 | |
| 26 | $100.00 | $2,800.00 | | 52 | $50.00 | $5,000.00 | |

## ACCOUNT INFORMATION

BANK NAME:

ACCOUNT TYPE:

ACCOUNT WEBSITE:                              BANK WEBSITE:

BANK TELEPHONE:

USERNAME:                                     PASSWORD:

# $10,000 YEARLONG SAVINGS CHALLENGE

| WEEK | DEPOSIT | TOTAL | ✓ | WEEK | DEPOSIT | TOTAL | ✓ |
|------|---------|-------|---|------|---------|-------|---|
| 1 | $193.00 | $193.00 | | 27 | $193.00 | $5,211.00 | |
| 2 | $193.00 | $386.00 | | 28 | $193.00 | $5,404.00 | |
| 3 | $193.00 | $579.00 | | 29 | $193.00 | $5,597.00 | |
| 4 | $193.00 | $772.00 | | 30 | $193.00 | $5,790.00 | |
| 5 | $193.00 | $965.00 | | 31 | $193.00 | $5,983.00 | |
| 6 | $193.00 | $1,158.00 | | 32 | $193.00 | $6,176.00 | |
| 7 | $193.00 | $1,351.00 | | 33 | $193.00 | $6,369.00 | |
| 8 | $193.00 | $1,544.00 | | 34 | $193.00 | $6,562.00 | |
| 9 | $193.00 | $1,737.00 | | 35 | $193.00 | $6,755.00 | |
| 10 | $193.00 | $1,930.00 | | 36 | $193.00 | $6,948.00 | |
| 11 | $193.00 | $2,123.00 | | 37 | $193.00 | $7,141.00 | |
| 12 | $193.00 | $2,316.00 | | 38 | $193.00 | $7,334.00 | |
| 13 | $193.00 | $2,509.00 | | 39 | $193.00 | $7,527.00 | |
| 14 | $193.00 | $2,702.00 | | 40 | $193.00 | $7,720.00 | |
| 15 | $193.00 | $2,895.00 | | 41 | $193.00 | $7,913.00 | |
| 16 | $193.00 | $3,088.00 | | 42 | $193.00 | $8,106.00 | |
| 17 | $193.00 | $3,281.00 | | 43 | $193.00 | $8,299.00 | |
| 18 | $193.00 | $3,474.00 | | 44 | $193.00 | $8,492.00 | |
| 19 | $193.00 | $3,667.00 | | 45 | $193.00 | $8,685.00 | |
| 20 | $193.00 | $3,860.00 | | 46 | $193.00 | $8,878.00 | |
| 21 | $193.00 | $4,053.00 | | 47 | $193.00 | $9,071.00 | |
| 22 | $193.00 | $4,246.00 | | 48 | $193.00 | $9,264.00 | |
| 23 | $193.00 | $4,439.00 | | 49 | $193.00 | $9,457.00 | |
| 24 | $193.00 | $4,632.00 | | 50 | $193.00 | $9,650.00 | |
| 25 | $193.00 | $4,825.00 | | 51 | $193.00 | $9,843.00 | |
| 26 | $193.00 | $5,018.00 | | 52 | $193.00 | $10,036.00 | |

## ACCOUNT INFORMATION

| | | |
|---|---|---|
| BANK NAME: | | |
| ACCOUNT TYPE: | | |
| ACCOUNT WEBSITE: | | BANK WEBSITE: |
| BANK TELEPHONE: | | |
| USERNAME: | | PASSWORD: |

# SUBSCRIPTION TRACKER

| SUBSCRIPTION NAME: | |
| --- | --- |
| SUBSCRIPTION START DATE | |
| WEBSITE | |
| USERNAME | |
| PASSWORD | |
| MONTHLY CHARGE | |
| CHARGE DATE | |
| SUBSCRIPTION NAME: | |
| SUBSCRIPTION START DATE | |
| WEBSITE | |
| USERNAME | |
| PASSWORD | |
| MONTHLY CHARGE | |
| CHARGE DATE | |
| SUBSCRIPTION NAME: | |
| SUBSCRIPTION START DATE | |
| WEBSITE | |
| USERNAME | |
| PASSWORD | |
| MONTHLY CHARGE | |
| CHARGE DATE | |
| SUBSCRIPTION NAME: | |
| SUBSCRIPTION START DATE | |
| WEBSITE | |
| USERNAME | |
| PASSWORD | |
| MONTHLY CHARGE | |
| CHARGE DATE | |

# DEBT

## PAYMENT TRACKER

| DEBT | | | |
|---|---|---|---|
| PAYMENT DUE DATE | | | |
| INTEREST RATE | | | |
| STARTING BALANCE | | | |
| PAYOFF DATE | | | |
| **PAYMENT DATE** | **PAYMENT AMOUNT** | **ADDED INTEREST** | **BALANCE** |
| | | | |
| | | | |
| | | | |
| | | | |
| | | | |
| | | | |
| | | | |
| | | | |
| | | | |

| DEBT | | | |
|---|---|---|---|
| PAYMENT DUE DATE | | | |
| INTEREST RATE | | | |
| STARTING BALANCE | | | |
| PAYOFF DATE | | | |
| **PAYMENT DATE** | **PAYMENT AMOUNT** | **ADDED INTEREST** | **BALANCE** |
| | | | |
| | | | |
| | | | |
| | | | |
| | | | |
| | | | |
| | | | |
| | | | |
| | | | |

# DEBT

| DEBT | | | |
|---|---|---|---|
| PAYMENT DUE DATE | | | |
| INTEREST RATE | | | |
| STARTING BALANCE | | | |
| PAYOFF DATE | | | |
| **PAYMENT DATE** | **PAYMENT AMOUNT** | **ADDED INTEREST** | **BALANCE** |
| | | | |
| | | | |
| | | | |
| | | | |
| | | | |
| | | | |
| | | | |
| | | | |
| | | | |

| DEBT | | | |
|---|---|---|---|
| PAYMENT DUE DATE | | | |
| INTEREST RATE | | | |
| STARTING BALANCE | | | |
| PAYOFF DATE | | | |
| **PAYMENT DATE** | **PAYMENT AMOUNT** | **ADDED INTEREST** | **BALANCE** |
| | | | |
| | | | |
| | | | |
| | | | |
| | | | |
| | | | |
| | | | |
| | | | |
| | | | |
| | | | |
| | | | |

# DEBT

| DEBT | | | |
|---|---|---|---|
| PAYMENT DUE DATE | | | |
| INTEREST RATE | | | |
| STARTING BALANCE | | | |
| PAYOFF DATE | | | |
| **PAYMENT DATE** | **PAYMENT AMOUNT** | **ADDED INTEREST** | **BALANCE** |
| | | | |
| | | | |
| | | | |
| | | | |
| | | | |
| | | | |
| | | | |
| | | | |

| DEBT | | | |
|---|---|---|---|
| PAYMENT DUE DATE | | | |
| INTEREST RATE | | | |
| STARTING BALANCE | | | |
| PAYOFF DATE | | | |
| **PAYMENT DATE** | **PAYMENT AMOUNT** | **ADDED INTEREST** | **BALANCE** |
| | | | |
| | | | |
| | | | |
| | | | |
| | | | |
| | | | |
| | | | |
| | | | |
| | | | |
| | | | |

# CONCLUSION

Congratulations! Whether you are a big family or small, young parents or empty nesters, a single parent, or simply single, you have now completed the process to bring unity and organization to your home. It's time to celebrate!

Just as a company puts workable systems in place to ensure a successful return on investment, your home is your business. You must maintain systems within it to ensure a great return and create a home that's filled with happiness and less stress—one that's designed for beautiful living.

If I could share one final piece of advice with you, it would be to make sure you are consistent with your family home meetings moving forward. These will keep the lines of communication open and strong within your family. If you maintain good family communication, then everything else will fall into place.

I wish you the best of luck as you continue your journey to a beautifully organized home!

# ACKNOWLEDGMENTS

If there's one thing I am sure of, it's that God never left my side during the writing of this book. He never leaves me no matter what I am doing in life, and I am forever thankful to Him.

I am also thankful that He gave me my wonderful husband, Mike. When I told Mike I was going to write this companion to *Beautifully Organized*, he immediately supported me. His genuine encouragement was what I needed to complete this book.

I would also like to thank my family, especially my mother and father. They are my cheerleaders and biggest supporters. I love you and thank you for being my rock!

I also have the best team a girl can have. They get my creative craziness and knew just what to do to support me as I wrote this book. Hazel, Becky, Brooke, Angela, Kate, Shakera, and Victoria: thank you for your dedication to my success.

To my Paige Tate & Co family, working with you is a writer's dream. Thanks for supporting me through the process of writing this book.

Thanks also to Cas for writing the foreword. You are simply amazing! You have a knack for putting a smile on my face, and on millions of others. I am honored to share a piece of your radiance in this book.

Finally, to all my friends: thank you for always being supportive. It means the world to me, and I am forever grateful that our paths have crossed.